Sustainable ESCAPES

CONTENTS

THE RISE OF SUSTAINABLE TRAVEL

Until recently, most travellers planned their adventures based on the most affordable and comfortable way to meet their travel goals, without giving much thought to how their choices might affect the destination. But priorities have begun to shift. On top of having a great time, travellers increasingly want to do the right thing by the places they visit.

What sustainable travel actually means and how to nail it, however, is still not widely understood. According to the World Tourism Organization, sustainable tourism is that which 'takes full account of its current and future economic, social and environmental impacts, addressing the needs of visitors, the industry, the environment and host communities.' In a nutshell, it's tourism that delivers meaningful guest experiences and benefits locals without negatively influencing communities and the environment. It works hand-in-hand with responsible travel in that sustainability is the goal, which travellers can help achieve by making more conscious travel decisions on the road.

While the term first emerged at the turn of the 21st century, it wasn't until the UN declared 2017 the International Year of Sustainable Tourism for Development that the concept of sustainable tourism really gained traction. Travellers began asking questions about the sustainability of traditionally popular travel experiences, and the industry has been forced to evolve in line with consumer attitudes. But while the global tourism industry has made great strides towards sustainability in recent years, achieving sustainable tourism is a continuous process. This process is reflected in our book. When we asked travel writers from around the globe to tell us about their favourite sustainable travel accommodation and experiences, their top picks covered the spectrum of sustainability. Some options had sustainability at heart from conception, while others have made a concerted effort to improve. What unites them, is a commitment to enacting positive change.

The sustainable escapes featured in our book prove that sustainable tourism is possible anywhere, and can take many forms, from high-end private island hideaways in Indonesia to intrepid coastal clean-up expeditions in Australia, and from remastered heritage hotels in Monaco to innovative community tourism projects in Cuba.

Don't know where to start? Our five chapters will help you navigate the vast choice of sustainable escape out there. Each corresponds to the key theme of the escape: Nature, Relaxation, Culture, Urban and Learning. Within each chapter, the profiles are labelled with the key sustainability features you can enjoy while staying at the hotel or participating in the tour – be they wildlife spotting, sustainable dining, homestays, expert talks, and more. The On Your Doorstep feature provides tips on sustainable tourism options beyond the location itself, while the practicalities panel provides the information you need to book it.

We hope that this book will prompt you to take stock of your travel habits, and inspire you to choose travel experiences that create incredible memories, while also helping to safeguard our fragile planet.

INNOVATIVE SUSTAINABLE TOURISM ATTRACTIONS AROUND THE WORLD

COPENHILL, DENMARK

Urban ski slopes typically take the form of emissions-emitting indoor centres. But not Copenhill. Opened in 2019, this artificial ski slope sits atop Amager Bakke, a waste-to-power plant central to Copenhagen's goal of becoming the world's first carbon-neutral city. The complex also has a 280ft (85m) climbing wall (the world's highest), and like all good ski resorts, an après-ski bar. // WWW.COPENHILL.DK

TABLE MOUNTAIN CABLEWAY, SOUTH AFRICA

Hiking Table Mountain is a quintessential Cape Town experience. But those who prefer to ride the cable car can still feel good about it. The cableway has been carbon-neutral since 2016, and maintains one of the most cohesive responsible tourism policies around.
// WWW.TABLEMOUNTAIN.NET

AZURMENDI, SPAIN

Proving it's haute to be sustainable, this three-Michelin-star restaurant near Bilbao has twice won the sustainable restaurant award from World's 50 Best Restaurants. The hilltop atrium building harnesses solar and geothermal energy, and guests can tour the on-site greenhouses and vegetable gardens that supply the inventive menus.
// WWW.AZURMENDI.RESTAURANT

CLIMATE MUSEUM, USA

It might not have a permanent home yet, but New York's Climate Museum has won a legion of fans for its innovative public exhibitions and events hosted around the city since 2017, from youth spoken-word programmes dedicated to themes of climate change to Climate Signals, a public art installation by US artist Justin Brice Guariglia, which flashed climate change alerts in five languages. // WWW.CLIMATEMUSEUM.ORG

JEWEL AT CHANGI, SINGAPORE

First came Gardens by the Bay with its solar-harvesting Supertrees, and in 2019 Singapore upped its urban garden game with an airport terminal you'll never want to leave. Harnessing cutting-edge sustainable technology, Jewel at Changi is a green oasis, complete with a hedge maze, a canopy bridge, and the world's tallest indoor waterfall. // WWW.JEWELCHANGIAIRPORT.COM

EDEN PROJECT, UK

Occupying the site of an excavated China clay pit, this education charity and visitor's centre in Cornwall, England, features huge biomes housing exhibitions, gardens and the largest rainforest in captivity. It's also home to the UK's longest and fastest zipline, and a play tower for kids designed to introduce little ones to the concept of pollination. // WWW.EDENPROJECT.COM

Top right: Jewel at Changi Airport, Singapore
Right: Changi's canopy bridge

OCEAN ATLAS, BAHAMAS

British sculptor and environmental activist Jason deCaires Taylor is famous for his surreal underwater sculptures that double as artificial reefs. Depicting a young girl supporting the ceiling of the water, much like the mythological Greek Titan shouldered the burden of the heavens, this 16-tonne sculpture in Nassau, was intended to symbolise the environmental burden we are asking future generations to carry. // WWW.UNDERWATERSCULPTURE.COM

BYRON BAY SOLAR TRAIN, AUSTRALIA

Connecting the centre of the New South Wales surf town to a vibrant arts estate, the world's first solar-powered train made its maiden journey on a scenic 3km stretch of disused rail line in 2017. In lieu of ticket machines, fares are collected by a conductor on the beautifully refurbished heritage diesel train.
// WWW.BYRONBAYTRAIN.COM.AU

WUNDERLAND KALKAR, GERMANY

Following the 1986 Chernobyl disaster, German authorities decided not to put its new multi-billion-euro nuclear reactor near the Dutch border into operation. But it wasn't a complete write-off. In the 1990s, the site was transformed into an amusement park, complete with a swing ride inside the reactor's cooling tower.
// WWW.WUNDERLANDKALKAR.EU

VENA CAVA, MEXICO

It calls itself the hippest winery in Mexico, and when you lay eyes on this all-organic Baja winery – which was constructed from reclaimed fishing boats and other recycled materials – it's difficult to disagree. Better yet, its cellar door is open for tastings every day of the week.
// WWW.VENACAVAWINE.COM

TIJ OBSERVATORY, NETHERLANDS

Taking its form from a tern's egg, this stunning public birdwatching observatory in Scheelhoek Nature Reserve in Stellendam was designed to rest as lightly on nature as possible. Built with sustainable wood and clad in thatched reeds, the observatory is reached via a tunnel built from recycled bulkheads to minimise disturbance to birds. // WWW.NATUURMONUMENTEN.NL

THE SAUNA IN FRIHAMNEN, SWEDEN

The city of Lund might be getting a bicycle-powered museum in 2024, but there's another great eco-friendly Swedish attraction you can visit now. Part of Jubileumsparken, the ongoing redevelopment of a Gothenburg port area into an ultra-sustainable leisure hub, this striking free public sauna was constructed largely from recycled materials. Be sure to check out the changing rooms, which were made from 12,000 recycled plastic bottles. // WWW.ALVSTADEN. GOTEBORG.SE/JUBILEUMSPARKEN

Clockwise from above: Byron Bay Solar Train; Wunderland Kalkar's swing ride; the epic view from Cape Town's Table Mountain Cableway

- Wildlife Watching
- Outdoor Adventure
- Conservation

NATURE

ARGENTINA

Awasi Iguazu

● *Spot over 400 bird species and maybe a jaguar, ocelot or tapir* ● *Explore the Atlantic Rainforest jungle with indigenous Guarani tribes* ● *See Iguazú Falls without the crowds*

Just 20 minutes' drive from South America's most recognised waterfall, this luxurious safari-style lodge situated on the banks of the Iguazú River is surrounded by the lush greenery of the Atlantic Rainforest, where the call of the region's plethora of birdlife – from green-billed toucans to magpie tanagers – ring throughout the foliage. Built on stilts for minimal environmental interference and positioned an easy walking distance from the main lodge, the property's 14 spacious villas are made of *petiribí* (an indigenous timber) and provide intimate access to the forest canopy of cassia and purple-flowering tibouchina trees, each replete with private living rooms, extensive decks with sun loungers and plunge pools, indoor-outdoor showers, and traditional textiles and baskets woven by the indigenous Guarani people.

With a private guide and a four-wheel drive vehicle included with each villa, guests have the luxury of tailor-making their exploration of the Atlantic Rainforest, where over 1000 species of endemic plants and wildlife thrive, from tropical orchids and ferns to capuchin monkeys and pumas. Awasi, which opened in 2018, worked with renowned biologists to create a series of excursions that go beyond the famous falls, including voyages to crystal-clear pools only accessible by boat, and visiting indigenous Guarani tribes to learn about

the importance of conservation in the area. Plus, guests get serious perks like entering Iguazú National Park from a secret location, allowing around 30 minutes of uninterrupted exploration before the crowds arrive.

ON YOUR DOORSTEP
Don't miss the opportunity to visit the nearby Mbya Guaraní settlement to meet the original inhabitants and guardians of Iguazú Falls and partake in nature walks to study wild medicinal plants. You can also join art classes to make works from clay and leaves.

$ *2-night stay all-incl per person from US$1900*

🍽 *Gourmet international cuisine featuring Atlantic Rainforest ingredients*

☞ **Selva Yriapú, Puerto Iguazú, Misiones; www. awasiguazu.com. Guests will be picked up in Puerto Iguazú by private guides**

AUSTRALIA

Lady Elliot Island Eco Resort

● *Snorkel and dive among huge manta rays* ● *Observe green and loggerhead turtles come ashore to nest* ● *Play an active role in regenerating the island*

With all of the Great Barrier Reef's resort islands offering incredible experiences, choosing between them isn't an easy task. For affordability and eco-friendliness, however, Lady Elliot Island is hard to beat. The southernmost coral cay of the Great Barrier Reef, this 43-room island resort has been recognised as one of the reef's leading ecologically sustainable tourism operators, providing guests with an opportunity to experience and learn about the island's unique ecosystem with minimal impact.

Known as the 'home of the manta ray', Lady Elliot is one of the best places in the world to hang out with these majestic filter feeders, while the island itself acts as an important nesting ground for seabirds and turtles, with the latter typically seen nesting between November and February.

To help preserve this natural wonder, the resort's current owners have implemented some of the region's most stringent eco-initiatives: banning plastic water bottles (the first resort on the reef to do so), purifying its own water, composting food waste and crushing glass bottles into sand. Its comfortable, mostly solar-powered rooms (including two glamping tents that opened in 2018) are fan-cooled, don't have TVs or phones, and are cleaned with biodegradable products.

Stripped of its vegetation by late-19th-century guano miners and goats placed on the island to feed shipwrecked sailors, the island has been painstakingly regenerated over the years, and guests keen to help are welcome to lend a hand in the on-site nursery. There's also a self-guided Climate Change Trail that highlights the effects of rising global temperatures on the reef, and suggests how visitors can help to mitigate their own influence.

$ *Doubles half-board per person AU$190*

🍽 *Breakfast and dinner buffets and pub-style lunches*

☞ **Queensland; www.ladyelliotisland. com.au. Lady Elliot Island is serviced by domestic flights from Hervey Bay, Bundaberg, Brisbane and the Gold Coast, all in Queensland**

AUSTRALIA

SWELL LODGE

● *Walk among millions of red crabs* ● *Hike to secret beaches and a hidden waterfall*
● *Learn how park rangers are working to save two lizard species*

It's better known for its detention centre, but from the moment you arrive on Christmas Island, a whopping 1550km off mainland Western Australia, you'll understand why those in-the-know refer to it as Australia's Galapagos. From its famous red crabs scuttling around everywhere to its majestic frigate birds riding the breeze, the island is the ultimate wildlife paradise. And thanks to the opening of Swell Lodge in 2018, there's now an incredible place to stay deep in its eponymous national park.

Perched on a clifftop overlooking the Indian Ocean – the water so clear parrotfish can be spotted dancing in the shallows – Swell Lodge isn't just the island's only luxury glamping accommodation, it's also the only place to stay in the national park. Built as eco-sensitively as possible, its two spacious solar-powered tents have composting toilets, eco-friendly toiletries, and not a single-use plastic amenity in sight. A 40-minute drive from town, it's an idyllic spot to recharge between adventures with your host, who will collect you each day for a rainforest hike, a snorkelling adventure, or perhaps a visit to the national park headquarters, where rangers are helping to save two endemic lizard species from extinction. Each evening, your personal chef will arrive to prepare a delicious three-course meal on your deck as the sun sets over the ocean, leaving

your breakfast in the fridge to serve yourself whenever the crashing waves rouse you.

ON YOUR DOORSTEP
From the lodge it's a 20-minute walk to secluded Merrial Beach, where you might be lucky enough to watch the annual red crab spawning that tends to occur in November or December. The lush Hugh's Dale Waterfall lies another 10 minutes' walk beyond.

$ *3-night stay incl meals and activities per person AU$2070*

🍽 *Creative gourmet meals garnished with island-foraged ingredients*

☞ *Christmas Island National Park, Christmas Island; www.swelllodge. com. You need to fly to Christmas Island from Perth or Jakarta. There's also a fortnightly flight from Kuala Lumpur. Your Swell Lodge host will meet you at the airport*

BOLIVIA
SERERE ECO RESERVE

● *Search the Amazon jungle for its famous wildlife* ● *Support the conservation work of a true Bolivian eco-warrior* ● *Choose your own outdoor adventure, based on your interests*

Rosa María Ruiz is a dominant figure in Bolivian conservation and one of the key people involved in creating the national park now known as Madidi, which is widely considered to be the protected area with the most biodiversity on the planet. Ruiz's vocal criticism of Madidi's level of protection under the government (and the rangers' inability to control illegal logging and hunting) resulted in death threats, the torching of her jungle lodge and an eventual ban from the very park she helped create. Undeterred, the wildlife warrior simply moved three hours' boat ride up the Beni River and set up her own 40-sq-km private wildlife reserve known as Serere.

Named after a bird with a blue face and punk-rock hair, this refuge in the Bolivian Amazon holds four steamy lagoons, a week's worth of hiking trails, and a wide variety of flora and fauna, including large troops of howler monkeys whose ethereal roars will become your morning alarm. When you visit the jungle camp at Serere you create your own itinerary based on your specific interests, with the help of indigenous guides. You eat organic food (much of which comes from the on-site garden) and sleep in spacious thatch-roofed cabins with screens for walls, so you feel like you're right in the thick of it when the tapirs saunter by. Stays here help fund Ruiz's ongoing conservation work across Bolivia.

ON YOUR DOORSTEP
When you return to Rurrenabaque, cross the Beni River to the town of San Buenaventura and visit the Centro Cultural Tacana. This is a great spot to browse local handicrafts and learn about the cosmovision of the indigenous Tacana people.

$ *3-day tour all-incl BOB1899*

🍽 *Family-style Bolivian meals with local Amazonian ingredients*

☛ *Rurrenabaque; www.madidi-travel. com. Serere is about 3 hours upriver from Rurrenabaque and rates include boat transfers*

BRAZIL

IBITIPOCA RESERVE

● *Explore a natural area where puma, maned wolf and ocelot roam* ● *Hike, bike, and horseback ride through Brazil's biodiverse Atlantic Forest* ● *Work alongside locals to conserve endangered species*

Once a family farm, Ibitipoca Reserve was converted to a natural sanctuary in the 1980s to serve as a vital wildlife corridor with neighbouring Ibitipoca State Park, a vast forested expanse spanning more than 1000 hectares. The hotel was established nearly 30 years later in 2008 and the property was expanded to protect 5000 hectares of wilderness where myriad species (including 350 birds, maned wolf and woolly spider monkey) thrive. Its mission: to ensure a continuous stretch of Atlantic Forest – one of the most endangered, yet biodiverse natural areas left on Earth – remained connected.

Guests stay in Fazenda do Engenhol, a renovated 18th-century farmhouse built in 1715, or in two separate guest houses surrounded by greenery. There's also a private wine cellar and a sauna and Jacuzzi on the property, but with over 200km of trails to explore in Ibitipoca Reserve and the Atlantic Forest, a stay here is about getting outdoors. Your adventures include daily guided hikes to tucked-away caves and canyons accessible through deep, narrow valleys; and biking, horseback riding and expeditions to the area's 90-odd waterfalls. The best part? You can also opt to work alongside the local community on projects that encourage locals to interact with ecotourism, with the most vital projects serving to protect such endangered endemic species as brocket deer, wild boar, ocelots and pumas.

ON YOUR DOORSTEP

Guests can visit Ibitipoca State Park, a forested area with waterfalls, caves, and hiking trails just 6km from the property, or Ibitipoca Reserve's own community project 9km away in São José dos Lopes called Casa Arte e Vida, where locals learn to make and sell handcrafts and pottery.

$ *Doubles all-incl from US$690*

🍽 *Homemade Brazilian cuisine with a French twist*

☛ *Fazenda do Engenho, Conceição do Ibitipoca, Minas Gerais; www.ibiti. com. The lodge can help arrange your journey from your arrival point*

AMAZON IN CRISIS

Illegal logging continues to take a huge toll on the Brazilian Amazon, but while it's easy to think an individual can't make a difference, there are ways you can help. Reducing your use of paper, wood, oil and even beef can help to reduce the pressure on clearing forests, while supporting rainforest protection initiatives like the Rainforest Action Network's Protect an Acre programme (www.ran.org/issue/protect_an_acre) can help to empower rainforest people to resist destructive practices.

BRUNEI
Ulu Ulu Resort

● *Spot rare wildlife in the lush primary rainforest surrounding your low-impact lodge*
● *Hike jungle trails and climb high into the forest canopy*

Brunei is best known for its oil and gas wealth and ultra-conservative (and controversial) version of Islamic Sharia law, but few people know that the tiny sultanate in Borneo's northwest has done a spectacular job of preserving its natural habitats. Lowland dipterocarp rainforests, virtually untouched by human activity, carpet the gentle hills of the Temburong District, which is separated from the rest of the country by a sliver of the Malaysian state of Sarawak.

Accessible only by *temuai*, a traditional, shallow-draft longboat, Ulu Ulu Resort sits at the northern edge of 500 sq km Ulu Temburong National Park, which features extraordinary biodiversity. The resort's signature activity involves climbing 60m up into the jungle canopy, where creaky scaffolding offers intimate views of the treetops and their resident orchids, ferns, frogs and snakes. Birds and mammals are easiest to spot around sunrise and sunset, but even then you're more likely to hear Bornean gibbons and rhinoceros hornbills than to see them. Waterfall hiking, kayaking, river tubing, and night walks are also on offer during longer stays.

The resort – where the recycling, composting, energy-efficient lighting and plastic bottle ban ensures that environmental effects are minimal – has just 17 rooms, all built of dark hardwoods in a style reminiscent of 1920s Malaya. The absence of television, internet

$ *1-night stay for 2 incl meals and transfers BND$660*

····························

⦿l *Traditional Iban-style meals with locally sourced ingredients*

····························

☛ Ulu Temburong National Park; www. uluuluresort.com. Rates include van and boat transfers from the capital Bandar Seri Begawan to the resort (2-3 hours each way)

and mobile phone reception intensifies the jungle's teeming, fecund splendour.

ON YOUR DOORSTEP

The Iban longhouse village of Batang Duri, the gateway to the national park, also houses several tourist lodges. These include Sumbiling Eco Village, run by Borneo Guide (borneoguide. com) in cooperation with the local community.

CAMBODIA

CHI PHAT

● *Spot langurs, hornbills, and maybe elephants near your jungle base* ● *Trek into the rainforests of the Cardamom Mountains* ● *Plant a tree or visit a wildlife release station*

After the end of the Cambodian civil war, the people of Chi Phat – who live on the southeastern edge of the Cardamom Mountains, a globally important biodiversity hotspot – turned to illegal logging and wildlife trafficking to survive. Realising that the only way to end these environmentally destructive practices was to address the underlying cause, the Wildlife Alliance (wildlifealliance.org) decided to help the 630 families of Chi Phat transform their remote, riverside village into a community-based ecotourism (CBET) project. Today, former poachers use their knowledge of the jungle to lead treks, families host visitors in their homes, and locals earn a living wage providing boat and motorbike transport. Not only is visiting a great way to experience rural Khmer life and hospitality and discover the sublime beauty of the rainforest, but it also supports sustainable conservation in which local people have a stake.

Led by friendly local guides (most speak some English), activities include day hikes, mountain biking, kayaking, swimming, birdwatching by boat, stargazing cruises and Khmer cooking classes. Accommodation, which is basic, comes with mosquito nets and cold-water bucket showers; some rooms have private bathrooms.

Booking accommodation, outings and transport through Chi Phat's CBET office ensures prices are fair and service providers get gigs on a rotating basis; 80% of income goes to the guide or host, while 20% is invested in education and community infrastructure. Advance reservations are highly recommended, especially during high season (November to March).

ON YOUR DOORSTEP

Led by an experienced CBET guide, jungle treks lasting up to a week take you deep into the Cardamom Mountains, across one of Asia's last elephant corridors. Accommodation is in a hammock, with a jungle cook preparing delicious Khmer meals.

$ *Doubles from US$8*

....

🍽 *Home-cooked Khmer meals for just US$3*

....

☛ *Koh Kong Province; www. chi-phat.org. It's a scenic, adventurous ride by longtail boat (2 hours) or moto (motorbike taxi; around 45 minutes) from Andeung Teuk, which is linked by bus with Phnom Penh (5 hours) and Sihanoukville (around 3 hours)*

CAMBODIA

SHINTA MANI WILD

● *Bed down in a luxury tent after a day of high-octane jungle adventures*
● *Help to fund wildlife conservation through community empowerment*

Southeast Asia's fabulously over-the-top hotel designer Bill Bensley got a tip from Cambodian philanthropist and hotelier Sokoun Chanpreda that a vital 350-hectare wildlife corridor abutting the Kirirom and Bokor national parks was being opened up for investment. The pair secretly attended the land auction, scored the winning bid, and set out to save the forest from its triple threats of poaching, mining and logging. The result: a luxurious tented camp that uses its funds to support conservation, environmental education and community development.

It's said that not a single one of the area's lush teak, rosewood or ironwood trees was felled in the creation of Shinta Mani Wild, which features 15 theatrical tent-cottages strewn along the edge of the Tmor Rung River. Perhaps that's why you need to strap on a harness and zip through the canopy just to get here (the less intrepid can take a rugged 4X4 access road).

Sustainability is woven into every aspect of the hotel experience. At the restaurant, chefs work to protect indigenous herbs and plants (like the juicy jungle fruit *kuy*) from disappearing by showcasing their gastronomic value. Over in the wellness centre, all treatments use a range of natural and chemical-free products, while excursions run the gamut from mountain biking down dusty trails to kayaking narrow streams to searching the forest for rare orchids with expert naturalists who've graduated from Phnom Penh's Royal University. The resort also funds a dedicated Wildlife Alliance guard station, so you can play ranger for a day and get your adrenalin pumping on an anti-poaching patrol, helping to ensure resident elephants, leopards and gibbons roam freely.

$ *3 nights for 2 all-incl from US$7000*

ⓘ *Creative Khmer cuisine with foraged finds*

☛ **Prey Praseth; www.shintamaniwild. com. Rates include land transfers from either Phnom Penh or Sihanoukville (both under 3 hours)**

CANADA

POLAR BEAR VIEWING

● Observe the world's largest bears in their natural habitat ● Tour the tundra in low-impact buggies ● Get inspired to act on climate change by visiting the front line

On Hudson Bay in northern Manitoba, the town of Churchill has been dubbed the polar bear capital of the world. Among the town's first polar bear tour operators, Frontiers North Adventures offers experiences that enable guests to observe these majestic mammals in the wild in custom-built Tundra Buggies, while following policies to avoid disturbing the animals or damaging the tundra ecosystem.

Polar bears migrate through this remote region, primarily in October and November, waiting for their winter hunting grounds on Hudson Bay to freeze. Taking a tour with Frontiers North around this time offers a fantastic opportunity to see bears up close in an eco-friendly way. Staff are also reporting that the sea ice now freezes later in autumn and thaws earlier in the spring, which is affecting polar bears' migration, hunting, and breeding patterns, so signing up for a tour also means you'll witness the effects of climate change with your own eyes.

A family-owned business established in 1987, Frontiers North has partnered with Polar Bears International to contribute to and share polar bear observations and research and to educate guests about these creatures and their natural environment. The company also started Churchill's first recycling programme. To further protect the local wildlife, they've even lobbied the provincial government to stop issuing tourism permits in the Churchill region, despite these restrictions limiting the company's own growth.

ON YOUR DOORSTEP

Churchill offers a different kind of wildlife experience in the summer, when Beluga whales migrate into Hudson Bay. Frontiers North operates whale-watching tours along the Churchill River and its estuaries, paired with land-based explorations of the region's plant and animal life.

$ *4-day polar bear tour with Frontiers North Adventures (www.frontiersnorth. com) from CAD$3249*

⏀❙ *Tundra Buggy lunches and Canadian staples at local restaurants*

☛ Tours begin in Winnipeg, Manitoba, with options to fly (2.5 hours) or travel by train (44 hours) to the northern town of Churchill

WHAT ABOUT ANTARCTIC SEA ICE?

Ever wondered why the decline of Arctic sea ice receives more attention than the decline of Antarctic sea ice? Scientists monitor sea ice in both regions, but Arctic sea ice is more significant to understanding the global climate because more Arctic ice remains through the summer months, reflecting sunlight and cooling the planet.

CHINA

VINTREE GAOLIGONG TENTED RESORT

● *Wildlife viewing opportunities abound near this pioneering tented camp*
● *Take local-guided hikes on trails that once formed part of the Southern Silk Road*

Stretching 500km across southwest China from the Tibetan Plateau to the Indochina Peninsula, the Gaoligong Mountains are a hotbed of biodiversity. Home to half of the nation's wildlife, the lush setting also provides the backdrop to arguably China's most innovative glamping resort.

A decade in the making, Gaoligong Tented Resort was built with low-impact materials and construction techniques to ensure minimal environmental interference. Rather than chop down trees to build a road, for example, its owners opted to link the 14 tents to a series of communal spaces via a 1km elevated wooden boardwalk. With interiors furnished in a nod to the age of scientific expedition and discovery, it's easy to imagine yourself as an intrepid naturalist as you gaze over the subtropical rainforest panorama from your private deck.

Activities here are based around exploring the nearby Gaoligongshan National Nature Reserve with local guides, where twitchers will delight in the abundant birdlife, and commonly spotted mammals include the endangered Phayre's leaf monkey and flying squirrels.

Only discovered in 2017, the Skywalker hoolock gibbon is also a local resident, though visitors hoping to lock eyes on an endangered (and very cute) red panda would be wise to plan their trip during the summer months. With some hikes held on ancient trails once part of the Southern Silk Road, you can soak up a bit of history while you're at it.

ON YOUR DOORSTEP
Cultural experiences available in nearby villages include interactive traditional shadow puppet shows and paper parasol painting. You can also luxuriate in the abundant hot springs in the nearest town, Tengchong.

$ *Per 2-person tent per night incl meals and some activities CNY4180*

....

🍽 *Seasonal Chinese dishes*

....

☛ **Xiaodifang Village, Wuhe County, Yunnan Province; www.vinetreetents.com. From Tengchong, it's a 90-minute drive southeast to the camp. The resort can assist with booking transport**

● **Wildlife Watching** ● **Outdoor Adventure**

CROATIA

HOTEL LYRA

● *Enjoy easy access to Plitvice Lakes National Park's dazzling pools and waterfalls*
● *Track bears and wolves, and spy 120 species of birds along wooded trails*

The name Lyra, meaning harp, is an astrological nod to the dark skies beneath which this hotel slumbers, bordering Croatia's Unesco-listed Plitvice Lakes National Park. There's so little light pollution here that Northern Hemisphere constellations like the harp are keenly visible, especially when viewed through telescopes installed in Hotel Lyra's rooftop rooms and gardens (there are in-room manuals to guide visitors' stargazing, too).

Nature is a constant companion at Lyra. It sits in a wooded clearing, with Plitvice Lakes' emerald pools just 16km away. Hiking the park's spider's web of trails is greatly encouraged, and there's even a small chance of spotting a European brown bear, lynx or eagle. Further afield, the hotel runs daily tours to little-explored Una National Park in Western Bosnia, with opportunities for white-water rafting in its canyons.

Inside, this four-star design hotel has a distinctly Balkan flavour. Lyra opened in 2019 with a mission to gain Green Key status, but also to embrace a responsible tourism ethos by regenerating the local community, which still bears the scars of the Balkan War. A charitable foundation has been established to help locals rebuild damaged homes, and the hotel consciously employs people from different communities (including Bosnians from across

the border) in an effort to bring them together and facilitate cross-cultural unity. People from the surrounding villages were also invited to share their home recipes, now served in the hotel's restaurant. Food is sourced locally, handmade crafts are championed in its souvenir shops, and brandy made from local plums is offered as a traditional welcome drink. As the Croatians would say: *živjeli* (cheers!) to that.

$ *Doubles from €95*

⦿ *Traditional Croatian dishes*

☛ *Ličko Petrovo Selo 5; www.hotelplitvice. com. The hotel can arrange private transfers from Zadar, Zagreb or Split, or catch a bus to Plitvice Lakes and it will pick you up from there for free*

ECUADOR

MASHPHI LODGE, ECUADOR

● *Get a monkey's-eye-view of the forest from a Sky Bike* ● *Support research in this biodiversity hotspot* ● *Look out for hummingbirds, toucans and rare flycatchers*

A cloud forest hideaway, three hours and a world away from traffic-choked Quito, the award-winning Mashpi was built without chopping down a single tree. The groundbreaking structure was constructed from recycled steel and glass and designed to blend into its surroundings. The 24 rooms and public areas are spacious and stylish, decorated in wood and stone, with wall-to-wall windows that immerse you in lush greenery.

The Ecuadorean Chocó-Andean forest once stretched all the way from Panama to Peru, but deforestation from logging, mining and farming have reduced it to less than 10% of its original size. In 2001, Roque Sevilla – entrepreneur and visionary environmentalist – rescued a vast expanse of the cloud forest and created the Masphi Reserve, and it's still expanding. It's a biodiversity hotspot, with around 500 bird species, along with many undocumented insects, reptiles and mammals, which the on-site team of biologists are discovering, researching and cataloguing. There's a butterfly breeding garden and camera trap project, too.

Awake to a chorus of trills, chirrups and whoops and explore the numerous hiking trails in the company of the country's finest naturalist guides and local loggers-turned-spotters. Or, for a bird's-eye view of the forest, scale the 26m-high observation tower, take a vertigo-inducing ride on a Sky Bike for two and board The Dragonfly, an open cable car. Back at the lodge, take a dip in the al fresco hot tub as wisps of cloud swirl around you or relax in the spa with a nature-inspired treatment, or take a yoga session. Evenings bring entertaining and informative presentations in the Expedition Room, delicious Ecuadorean-inspired dishes in the double-height, glass-fronted restaurant, and relaxed chat in Explorers' Bar over creative cocktails.

$ *Doubles all-incl from US$1340*

🍽 *Homemade Brazilian cuisine with a French twist*

☛ **Reserva Privada Mashpi; www. mashpilodge.com. Mashpi arranges shared transfers from the Ecuadorean capital Quito**

ECUADOR

Pikaia Lodge

● *Stay in luxury rooms and suites within a private wild giant tortoise reserve*
● *Explore the Galápagos Islands by private yacht*

Perched on the edge of two extinct volcanic craters above the second largest protected marine reserve on Earth, Pikaia Lodge offers the ultimate low-impact, land-based option for experiencing the Galápagos Islands. When it opened in 2014, the lodge launched an ambitious reforestation project by planting 12,000 endemic trees, which in turn enticed the wild giant tortoise to return to the area. Now protecting a 31-hectare reserve where the species thrives, the lodge offers easy access not just to wild tortoises but to the secluded white-sand beaches and wildlife hotspots of Galápagos

National Park, which are accessible without the need to sign up for a multi-day cruise.

Completely carbon neutral and built with roofing designed to collect rainwater to be purified by reverse osmosis, Pikaia Lodge's 14 luxurious rooms and suites have expansive shaded terraces with views of the Pacific Ocean or the verdant hills of Galápagos National Park. Not that you're likely to spend much time in them, as a stay here is all about exploring the natural wonders of the Galápagos in style. Offering comfort, privacy, and fine dining on its half- and full-day tours, the lodge also has its own fleet of private yachts for day cruises to such nearby islands as North Seymour, where blue-footed boobies and magnificent frigate birds nest in the thousands, and the Plaza Islands, where bright yellow land iguanas feast on cacti near colonies of sea lions resting on sandy rocks. Framed by plush beach chairs, the central infinity pool is a fine place to while away an afternoon after a busy morning of adventures, while a covered terrace sets the scene for fine, multi-course dining.

ON YOUR DOORSTEP
Guests can visit the Charles Darwin Research Station on Santa Cruz Island to learn how scientists protect the Galápagos Islands by advising locals and visitors on how to conserve the archipelago and its endemic species.

$ *3-night stay all-incl per person from $4680*

⦿| *Gourmet Ecuadorian fusion*

☞ *Isla Santa Cruz, Galápagos Islands; www.pikaialodge. com. Pikaia Lodge is reached by a 2-hour flight from Guayaquil on mainland Ecuador to Galápagos Baltra Airport, where guests will be escorted to the property*

FINLAND
Nolla – The Zero Cabin

● *Stay in a Scandi-cool zero-waste cabin that funds ocean clean-up initiatives* ● *Explore wildflower meadows, dense forests and waterfront views in the heart of the Finnish Archipelago*

The perfect combination of no-frills camping and effortless Scandinavian cool, Nolla – The Zero Cabin is a compact wooden A-frame structure perched on the western shore of Vallisaari Island, part of the Finnish Archipelago. Housing two cosy camping beds and a small kitchen, with bathroom facilities a short walk away, the entirely mobile cabin was designed by Finnish architect Robin Falck to have the smallest environmental footprint possible. Part of a sustainability initiative by Neste (a Finnish sustainable fuels producer), it's intended to provide visitors with a minimalist and harmonious experience in nature. Powered entirely by solar energy and renewable fuels, the cabin generates zero emissions and demonstrates a modern sustainable hospitality solution brought to life with signature Scandinavian aesthetics. Best of all, proceeds are donated to The Ocean Cleanup non-profit organisation, which develops advanced technologies to rid the world's oceans of plastic.

ON YOUR DOORSTEP
Vallisaari is a former military island closed to the public until 2016. It's now a popular destination for locals and tourists, revered for its biodiversity and 19th-century military fortifications dating back to the Crimean war.

$ *Cabin per night bookable via www. airbnb.com €30*

🍽 *Cook your own zero-waste meals*

☛ *Vallisaari Island, Helsinki. Vallisaari is 10 minutes from central Helsinki and served by ferries in summer*

GREENLAND

EAST GREENLAND BASE CAMP

● Tread lightly in one of the world's most remote wilderness areas ● Face-off with climate change in the Arctic ● Look out for whales and seals on a zodiac tour

With technology making the furthest corners of our planet more accessible every year, it's becoming increasingly difficult to truly get off the beaten track. And that's exactly what makes Natural Habitat Adventures' Greenland base camp so special.

Known for its pioneering sustainable tourism initiatives – such as becoming the world's first carbon-neutral travel company in 2007 and hosting the world's first zero-waste organised tour in 2019 – the US-based adventure travel operator approached the construction of its luxury safari camp in East Greenland, one of the most remote places on Earth, with the deepest respect for the fragile environment. In operation for just two months each summer, the eight-room tented camp is dismantled for the rest of the year to further minimise its impact. With solid waste hauled out to the nearest responsible disposal facility and only biodegradable soap used in the kitchen and bathrooms, nothing is left behind.

With incredible views towards the Greenland ice sheet, the atmospheric camp, which has a central yurt for naturalist presentations and lounging, acts as a base for exploring the vast, pristine wilderness of East Greenland over four days of Natural Habitat Adventures' nine-day Discover Greenland tour. With daily hikes, kayak trips, and zodiac rides

giving travellers a first-person perspective of climate change in action, it's the kind of trip that changes you – for the better.

ON YOUR DOORSTEP
The camp is located near the tiny hamlet of Tinit, offering guests an opportunity to connect with Inuit culture and learn how climatic changes are affecting the lives of locals, who live a subsistence lifestyle amid the constantly shifting ice.

$ *9-day Discover Greenland tour with Natural Habitat Adventures (www. nathab.com) all-incl except internal flights per person US$12,995*

....

🍽 *Hearty international fare*

....

☞ **Tours begin in Reykjavik, Iceland**

7 TIPS FOR RESPONSIBLE WILDLIFE INTERACTIONS

As the dark truths behind many wildlife tourism activities become clearer, the case for choosing more responsible (and as a result, more sustainable) options has never been stronger. Learning what this means, and putting it into practice, is key.

'The important thing to keep in mind is that wild animals are not entertainers,' says Ben Pearson, Senior Campaign Manager for the Australian branch of international animal welfare non-profit World Animal Protection. 'If you want to see wildlife on holiday, the best thing you can do is to find somewhere to see it in the wild. The next best option is seeking out a legitimate sanctuary that offers observation only, so the animals are free to display their natural behaviours.'

This might sound restrictive, but nothing elevates a wildlife experience like knowing that the animals involved are as comfortable to be in your presence as they make you happy to be in theirs. Follow these tips to ensure you don't upset the balance.

KEEP YOUR DISTANCE

'If a tourism venue offers the opportunity to ride, touch or get a selfie with a wild animal, there's every chance that animal has been treated cruelly,' says Pearson. Animal shows, elephant rides, captive dolphin swims, and interacting with big cats are more widely publicised examples of tourism experiences that compromise animal welfare, but even seemingly harmless interactions like visiting a hedgehog cafe can have devastating effects.

The alternative? Walking and vehicle safaris led by experienced guides offers the thrill of observing wildlife in its natural habitat, while keeping the animals – and you – safe.

SEEK OUT GENUINE SANCTUARIES

Wildlife sanctuaries provide valuable opportunities to view and learn about species that are difficult to spot in the wild, but it pays to do your research to ensure sanctuaries you plan on visiting are operating in the true sense of the term. On top of a no-contact policy, legitimate sanctuaries should have adequate enclosures. 'Check if the animals have room to move and display natural behaviours,' says Pearson. 'Is there protection from the weather and somewhere for them to get away from visitors?'

RESIST THE URGE TO FEED WILDLIFE

Despite your best intentions, feeding wildlife can do more harm than good.

'As a result of continued feeding, animals become dependent on humans for food, and can become aggressive,' says Pearson. Feeding wildlife can also make animals sick, and wreak havoc with their breeding and migration patterns.

BEWARE OF GREY AREAS

Be mindful that so-called sustainable alternatives to problematic activities often have their own issues.

'Elephant washing is a big one,' says Pearson. 'Many people believe this is a better alternative to riding, but allowing tourists to wash an elephant requires a high level of control over the animal. With mud used as sun protection, this constant washing can have a negative impact on their welfare, too.'

WATCH WHAT YOU EAT

'Avoid things like bush meat, which is often hunted and killed inhumanely,' says Pearson. And don't forget your drinks. Snake wine, for example, is typically made by drowning a live snake in alcohol, while coffee luwak is produced by caging and force-feeding civet cats.

SHOP WISELY

Avoiding souvenirs made from wild animals such as traditional medicines and coral jewellery is also part of being a responsible wildlife tourist.

'Instead,' says Pearson, 'buy locally produced, environmentally sustainable souvenirs. You'll be supporting local communities and culture, and protecting animals, too.'

SPEAK UP

'Raising awareness of poor animal treatment is one of the best things you can do to stop it,' says Pearson, who suggests respectfully raising the issue with the venue, and sharing your experience with friends and family via social media.

'We know most people partake in wildlife tourism experiences because they love animals. If more people are aware of the impact on wildlife welfare before they book their trip, they're less likely to partake in problematic activities.'

3 DOCUMENTARIES TO WATCH BEFORE YOUR NEXT WILDLIFE HOLIDAY

- *Love & Bananas* (Ashley Bell; 2018): The practice of keeping Asian elephants captive for tourism is examined in this film.

- *Blood Lions* (Bruce Young & Nick Chavallier; 2015): The link between Africa's canned hunting and tourism industries is exposed in this difficult-to-watch flick.

- *Blackfish* (Gabriela Cowperthwaite; 2013): The gripping documentary that put the spotlight on the cruelty of keeping cetaceans in captivity.

GUYANA
Surama Ecolodge

● *Spot giant otter, tapir and more on a river paddle near your jungle lodge*
● *Keep your eyes peeled for 500 bird species on a guided hike*

With more than 80% of its territory blanketed by thick jungle and a number of international donors helping to ensure it stays that way, the small South American nation of Guyana (the continent's only English-speaking country) should be better known for its sustainable eco-tourism potential. While access to its steamy jungles remains a challenge, its community-owned-and-run eco-lodges make the journey well worth the effort.

Run by the Makushi Amerindian community in the country's heart, Surama Lodge is one of the most established. Featuring a range of simple but characterful accommodation options – from octagonal *benabs* (cottages) to hammocks – it's the perfect base for jungle exploration. Activities include wildlife-viewing hikes, river paddles and surveying the rainforest from the summit of a nearby mountain. With more than 500 species of birdlife found in the forest adjacent to the lodge, and local guides adept at spotting them, twitchers will be in absolute heaven.

With lodge activities accounting for around 60% of the community's income, your visit not only creates meaningful employment for

locals (reducing the incentive to abandon their home to mine or cut timber in other parts of Guyana), but an opportunity to soak up local life on the community's terms. Also used as a space for cultural performances, the main *benab* (where meals are served) is a good spot to enjoy a hearty dose of local arts.

ON YOUR DOORSTEP
The community also runs two more rustic camps on the Burro-Burro River where you can spot wildlife, fish for piranha, and string up your hammock and doze off to the chorus of the jungle.

$ *4-day nature-focused visit all-incl per person US$473*

🍽 *Guyanese flavours*

☛ **Surama, North Rupununi; https://suramaecolodge.com. The 30-minute flight from Georgetown to the Surama airstrip with TransGuyana Airways costs around US$300 return. The cheaper overland alternative is around 12 hours**

INDIA

FORSYTH LODGE

● *Try your luck spotting tigers, sloth bears and more on a jeep safari guided by a passionate naturalist* ● *Take a stroll in India's only tiger park that allows walking safaris*

Known as India's 'Tiger State', Madhya Pradesh is arguably the best place on the planet to try your luck at spotting one of the 3000-odd Bengal tigers thought to remain in the wild. While Kanha and Bandhavgarh are the stars of the central Indian state's tiger parks, Satpura National Park offers a wider range of activities to help take pressure off the park's core zone, and arguably your best shot of spotting a sloth bear.

Hidden in reclaimed jungle in the park's buffer zone, Forsyth Lodge is the most sustainable-luxe base you could want. A member of the UN-backed sustainable tourism certification scheme Tour Operators for Tigers, the lodge's 12 cottage-style guest rooms were built via the natural cob method, which helps to naturally moderate the temperature throughout the seasons. Single-use plastics are out, as are TVs and wi-fi, encouraging guests to mingle around the pool or at the open-air terrace bar in the main building.

Led by some of India's most experienced and passionate naturalists, activities are centred in the park, with canoe and walking safaris (as well as a camping and a junior ranger programme) offered alongside jeep safaris. Accounting for 80% of lodge staff, the local community also plays an active role in wildlife conservation via an incentive programme for reporting wildlife activity. With no fences around the lodge

itself, you might even spot deer, wild boar, or even a wildcat wandering the grounds.

ON YOUR DOORSTEP
Break up your transfer to or from Bhopal with a pit-stop at the Rock Shelters of Bhimbetka, located roughly halfway. Exhibiting the earliest traces of human life on the Subcontinent, these Unesco-listed rock art galleries are surprisingly well preserved.

$ *Doubles incl meals from INR22,077*

◯❘ *Gourmet organic Indian and international dishes*

☛ **Bija Kheri, Soghapur, Madhya Pradesh; www. forsythlodge.com. Forsyth Lodge is 4 hours' drive south of Bhopal. Transfers can be arranged through the lodge**

KENYA

OL PEJETA CONSERVANCY

● Ride horses among rhinos while staying at a cattle ranch-turned eco-camp ● Track and identify lions for research purposes ● Spot aardvarks, bat-eared foxes and nocturnal hunts on night drives

This former colonial cattle ranch on Kenya's Laikipia Plateau (the savannah grasslands stretching from Mount Kenya to the rim of the Great Rift Valley) has been transformed into East Africa's largest black rhino sanctuary. Home to the last two recorded northern white rhinos (a mother and daughter) and a Jane Goodall Institute-affiliated chimpanzee sanctuary with Kenya's only chimps, the 365 sq km conservancy also has some of the country's highest predator densities and a livestock program.

Ol Pejeta's current chapter began in 2004, when British conservation NGO Fauna & Flora International and the Arcus Foundation charity, established by US philanthropist Jon Stryker, purchased the land to rehabilitate animals rescued from the black market. Now a Kenyan-owned operation with a management plan drawn up by staff and a focus on local community development, it's one of just three sub-Saharan conservancies with Green List status, awarded for excellent management of valuable natural areas.

Ol Pejeta innovations include deploying drones to track poachers, while activities at the Big Five reserve range from classic game drives to eco-friendly experiences including safaris on horseback, on bikes, and on foot. Guests are encouraged to get their khaki dirty on interactive tours, such as visiting the tracker dogs' kennels

$ *Camping per night per person from KES1000 plus US$90 daily conservancy fee*

|●| *Kenyan bush tucker*

☞ Nanyuki; www. olpejetaconservancy. org. Transfers are available from Nanyuki

and moving a predator-proof cattle enclosure. If you're not into camping, accommodation in cottages and a budget-friendly former stables is also available, with features such as solar power to minimise environmental effects.

ON YOUR DOORSTEP

Ol Pejeta is just over an hour's drive from the beginning of the popular three-day Naro Moru hiking route to Point Lenana (4985m), Mt Kenya's third-highest peak. Highly susceptible to climate change, the mountain's glaciers are estimated to be gone within 25 years.

KENYA

SARARA CAMP

● *Cool off in the infinity pool overlooking an elephant watering hole* ● *Explore the savannah with Samburu warriors* ● *Empower a local community to protect wildlife that roams their land*

Hugged by the jagged peaks of the Mathews Range in the heart of northern Kenya, Sarara Camp is a truly unique safari experience. Translating to 'meeting place' in the Samburu language, the eight-tent luxury camp is set within a diminutive portion of the vast 3440 sq km Namunyak Wildlife Conservancy and is entirely owned and managed by the Samburu community's 1200 families. Originally founded in 1997 by Kenyan-born conservation pioneers Piers and Hilary Bastard, Sarara Camp has grown from a mobile camp to a luxury eco-retreat with support from such organisations as Conservation International, which assists the Samburu in protecting one of the most vital stretches of untouched wilderness remaining on the African continent.

Lauded for their community-based conservation model, Sarara place equal emphasis on viewing wildlife and experiencing indigenous culture. With a Samburu warrior as your safari guide, you can explore the savanna on foot, where elephants, giraffes and dik-diks graze among forests of acacia and juniper. During cultural outings, you can join a circle of Samburu women to craft beaded jewellery or take a bush walk to the 'singing wells', where Samburu warriors continue the ancestral tradition of chanting songs as they gather their cattle to drink. After game drives, it's time for mingling over sundowners at the lodge's communal area perched atop a swimming pool that overlooks a watering hole frequented by elephants, giraffe and zebra.

ON YOUR DOORSTEP

Less than an hour's drive from Sarara is Reteti Elephant Sanctuary, Africa's first community-owned-and-managed elephant orphanage. Visitors can learn how the Samburu community cares for orphaned and abandoned elephant calves until their re-release into the wild.

$ *Doubles all-incl: US$1670*

⦿I *Contemporary international fare crafted from home-grown produce*

☛ **Namunyak Wildlife Conservancy; www. sararacamp.com**

KYRGYZSTAN

PROTECTING SNOW LEOPARDS IN TIEN SHAN

● *Spot rare Central Asian alpine wildlife on a scientific expedition* ● *Explore Kyrgyzstan's breathtaking alpine wilderness* ● *Survey rare snow leopards and their prey*

A region so beautiful it translates to 'Mountains of Heaven' in English, Kyrgyzstan's Tien Shan mountains also play home to one of the world's most elusive big cat species. On a scientific expedition with not-for-profit Biosphere Expeditions, you can try your luck at spotting a snow leopard in its natural habitat while also playing an active role in conserving the vulnerable species.

Led by an expedition leader and a scientist, 14-member trips (typically held three times annually) are based in comfortable mobile tented camps with bathroom facilities in the mountains, from where volunteers spend their days setting out on foot and in vehicles to look for tracks, kills, scats and the animals themselves. You'll also set and assess footage from camera traps, and work with the local anti-poaching patrol on conservation initiatives within the local community, with rest days to soak up the breathtaking location.

Claiming to be the world's only organisation with a direct and transparent link between the work done by citizen scientists and an expedition report, Biosphere Expeditions provides guests with a comprehensive report following the trip, with research gathered often cited in scientific publications. When the snow leopard population of Tien Shan has been identified, the company seeks to influence decision-makers in government towards the creation of protected areas. Adding to the feel-good factor, it's also one of the world's few tourism operators that offers vegetarian dishes wherever possible.

ON YOUR DOORSTEP
There's an option to pack a tent and camp out in an even more remote location to carry out intensive survey work; keep your eyes peeled for wildlife such as argali mountain sheep, Central Asian ibex, lynx, marmots and even bears and grey wolves.

$ *13-day Protecting Snow Leopards in Tien Shan expedition with Biosphere Expeditions (www.biosphere-expeditions.org) €2200*

⦿ *Hearty vegetarian meals*

☛ Participants will need to make their own way to the expedition joining point in the capital Bishkek, from where the group will travel to the Tien Shan Mountains

● **Wildlife Watching**   ● **Outdoor Adventure**   ● **Conservation**

LAOS

ELEPHANT CONSERVATION CENTER

● *Sleep on the edge of a lush forest where you can hang out with elephants in a responsible manner* ● *Support a breeding program backed by the Smithsonian Institution*

Get to know 29 Asian elephants as they bathe, feed and raise babies in a 530-hectare protected forest along the shores of the serene Nam Tien lake. On a one- or two-night stay at this highly respected conservation centre you'll sleep and eat in their midst while learning about the plight of elephants in Laos from a team of international vets and local guides. Longer seven-day volunteer stays go more in-depth as you help with current projects and assist in the caretaking of the animals.

Arriving at the Elephant Conservation Center (ECC) is a memorable experience as a small wooden boat glides through the green weeds that carpet Nam Tien lake. You then drop your belongings in either fan-cooled bungalows with shared bathrooms or the more comfortable rosewood lodge (a stilt house based on the traditional Tai Lue style).

The ECC houses the largest elephant herd under human care in Laos and has a strict no-riding policy for visitors. Most animals have been rescued from the logging industry, or have been brought here to aid in the centre's breeding program (the ECC hopes to re-create sustainable breeding populations in the wild). Your tourist dollars fund one of the last rays of hope for Laos' dwindling elephant population. There are just 400 of these pachyderms left in the wild, but with the ECC's help, the future could look a lot brighter.

ON YOUR DOORSTEP
Before you depart Luang Prabang for the centre, be sure to stop by Big Brother Mouse (bigbrothermouse.com), a home-grown publishing house that produces colourful Lao-language children's books, many of which depict local fairy tales.

$ *2-day experience incl meals and activities from US$210*

🍽 *Family-style Laotian meals with accessible spice levels*

☛ *Sainyabuli; www. elephantconservation center.com. Sainyabuli is 2½ hours southwest of Luang Prabang. Rates include minivan transfers to/ from Luang Prabang*

MALAWI

TONGOLE WILDERNESS LODGE

● *Paddle down the Bua River, spotting elephants, crocs and over 280 bird species*
● *Explore the bush on foot with an armed guide* ● *Help conserve cultural traditions*

Deep in the Nkhotakota Wildlife Reserve, one of Malawi's least developed wildernesses, Tongole Wilderness Lodge hugs the banks of the Bua River, which crosses this 1800 sq km of miombo woodland, rainforest and tall grasses en route to Lake Malawi. In the morning, guests can watch the sunshine warm the boulders in the river from the wooden deck or handmade sunken bath in their thatched suite, sustainably built to blend in with the environment using local materials. Alternatively, climb the floating staircase and mezzanine walkway to the crow's nest of a viewing platform, tucked beneath the church-high roof of the main lodge. You'll be back here for a sundowner, but before that there are canoe safaris, wildlife drives, mountain walking and village visits to choose between.

Tongole has won a mantelpiece of gongs in the global wildlife tourism industry's Safari Awards, including Best Ecologically Responsible, Best Community Focused and Best Value Safari Property in 2018. It began with the solar-powered lodge's two-year construction, which created 100 much-needed jobs for locals, and continues with the training and employment of 30-plus local staff. The lodge promotes low-impact river and walking safaris, and has established the Tongole Foundation charity to broaden its positive effect on the poor communities around the reserve. The

foundation's work includes repairing and maintaining three local schools, reducing poaching through education and employment, and distributing mosquito nets to prevent infant deaths from malaria and cholera.

ON YOUR DOORSTEP
Nkhotakota Wildlife Reserve recently received 520 elephants in a record-breaking translocation from two southern Malawian parks, along with over 1000 antelopes, buffaloes and warthogs. Spot some alongside crocs, giant kingfishers and black storks.

$ *Doubles per person all-incl US$455*

....

🍽 *Safari fuel with locally sourced ingredients*

....

☛ **Nkhotakota Wildlife Reserve; www.tongole.com. Self-driving (a 4WD) from the capital Lilongwe (230km, four hours) is easiest, but Tongole can collect guests from Nkhotakota town, served by taxis and the Lake Malawi Ilala ferry. Ulendo Airlink also serves the lodge**

MALAYSIA

PERHENTIAN TURTLE PROJECT

● *Identify and track turtles on snorkelling trips* ● *Get your turtle-viewing fix on a volunteering project designed to save them* ● *Help ensure turtle safety on anti-poaching patrols*

Four species of sea turtle make their homes in the tropical waters around Malaysia. However, a lethal combination of factors including poaching of eggs, collisions with boats, pollution and climate change have conspired to bring some turtle populations to the brink of extinction.

Aiming to halt the deadly tide on the northeast coast of Peninsular Malaysia is the Perhentian Turtle Project, one of the programmes run by Ecoteer, a voluntourism organisation founded by British marine biologist Daniel Quilter in 2005. Between April and September, Perhentian Kecil, the smaller of the two idyllic Perhentian Islands, is the base for the project monitoring the local population of green turtles.

In collaboration with local conservation groups, volunteers help to collect scientific data by snorkelling and taking photos of turtles. These photos are then used to identify individual turtles and their movements around the islands, which assists in creating a sea turtle management plan for the islands. There are also night-time duties of guarding the turtle nesting beaches against potential poachers.

In your free time, there's amazing snorkelling and diving to be had around the islands' coral reefs, while the islands themselves offer gentle jungle hiking to sandy beaches and to hilltop lookouts. Volunteers also get to experience local Malay village life, living communally in a guest lodge and taking turns to cook dinner once a week.

ON YOUR DOORSTEP

Another of Ecoteer's projects is the Perhentian Marine Research Station. It's possible to learn to dive with them, then volunteer your time to help with their research to protect the island's fragile coral reefs and seagrass beds.

$ *2-week volunteering project full board from US$890*

....

❍ *Tasty Malaysian fare*

....

☞ *Pulau Perhentian Kercil, Terengganu; www.ecoteer.com. From Kota Bharu take a taxi or bus to Kuala Besut (50km south), and then a boat to the Perhentians (30-40 minutes)*

MOZAMBIQUE
Casa Das Garças

● *Stay at a low-impact seaside guest house that doubles as an environmental research centre*
● *Hike through mangrove forests and snorkel atop dazzling reefs* ● *Spot dolphins from a kayak*

Casa Das Garças may seem like your average low-impact beachfront guest house, but there's so much more going on here than tasty local cooking and stand-up paddleboarding between the mangroves. Located on Ibo Island, one of the Mozambique's historical highlights, the characterful guest house was built in partnership with the international student-led non-profit Oikos. Part of the charity's mission is to create sustainable economic opportunities for Mozambicans – a majority of whom live below the poverty line – while protecting the country's threatened ecosystems. Casa Das Garças not only provides employment to locals but also hosts vocational training and serves as a basecamp for environmental researchers studying in the country. It was built with locally sourced materials and uses extensive rainwater collection systems to minimise its environmental effect as much as possible. Nature surrounds the lodge, so wildlife viewing opportunities abound, either from land or by boat.

ON YOUR DOORSTEP
Stop by the Silversmith Project at nearby Ibo Island Lodge (iboisland.com), where local artisans make silver jewellery using centuries-old designs and techniques. Taking a jewellery-making class is a great way to support traditional island arts.

$ *Doubles US$65*

⦿❘ *Light local and international fare*

☛ Rua da Fortaleza, Ibo Island; www. casadasgarcas.org. The hotel arranges boat transfers from Tandanhangue to Ibo Island

Mangroves of Mozambique

Eastern African mangroves provide a vital habitat for migratory birds, marine turtles, dugongs and dolphins. Despite facing various threats, the mangrove forests of Mozambique are so vast (totalling around 2% of the world's mangroves) that the country remains a great base for spotting these critters.

● Wildlife Watching ● Outdoor Adventure ● Conservation

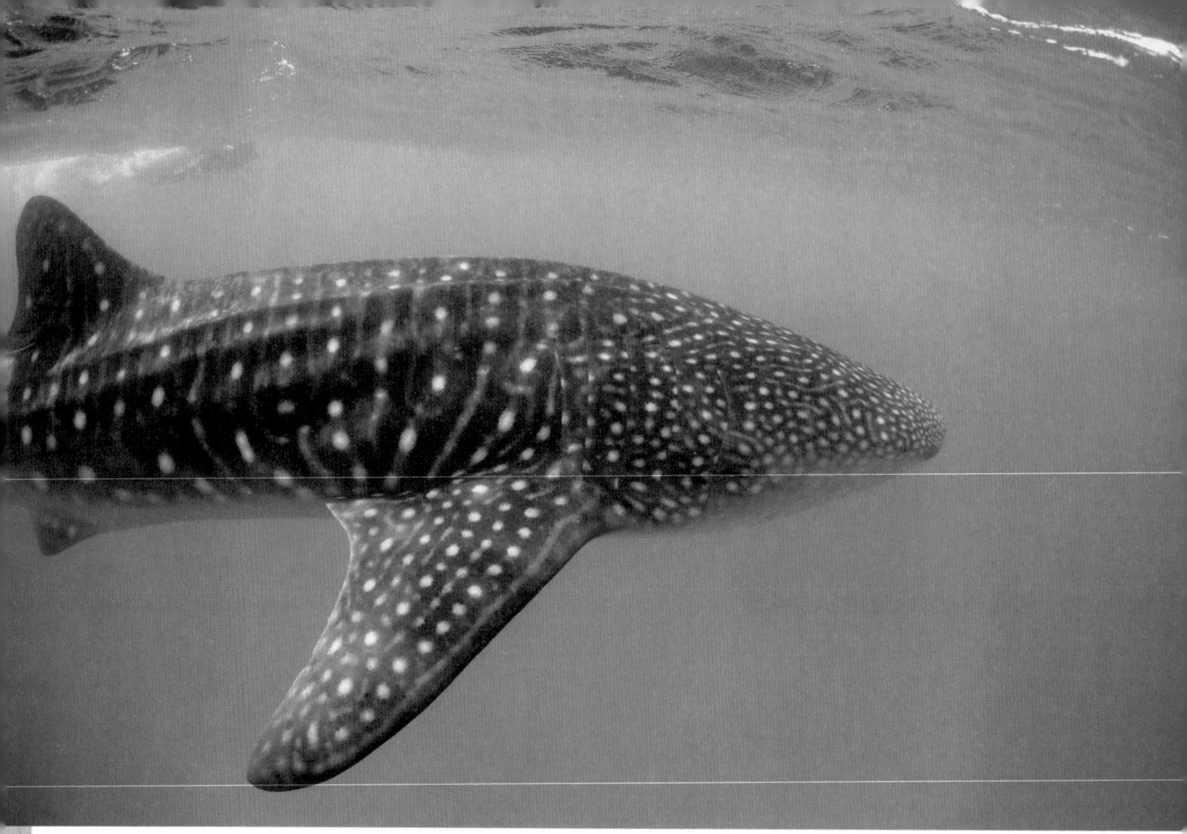

MOZAMBIQUE

Marine Conservation Expedition

● *Dive among whale sharks, manta rays, and maybe even humpback whales* ● *Explore Mozambique's dazzling coral reefs* ● *Photograph megafauna for scientific research*

Swimming with whale sharks has become a bucket-list travel experience, and you can't do it much more sustainably than on a scientific expedition with the Marine Megafauna Foundation (MMF). Focused on using pioneering research, education, and sustainable conservation solutions to protect marine life, the US non-profit launched its first expeditions in Mozambique – the home of its research base – in 2019, offering certified scuba divers an opportunity to be actively involved in the conservation of the marine life they dive with.

Over a week, participants log a dozen-odd dives around Tofo (aka the whale shark capital of Africa) and the Bazaruto Archipelago, during which they'll assist MMF marine biologists in building a photographic catalogue of marine life encountered. Eco-minded accommodation sets the scene for evenings of scientific presentations, offering additional opportunities to soak up the knowledge of marine experts.

ON YOUR DOORSTEP

Step behind Tofo's party scene on a Tofo Life (facebook.com/tofolife) community tour. Set up and run by 10 local women, the project helps reduce their dependence on fishing for their livelihood.

$ *8-night expedition incl diving per person from US$3280; www.marinemegafaunafoundation.org*

International/local

The tour begins in Tofo, 500km northeast of the capital Maputo. Daily buses make the 7½-hour journey

NAMIBIA

DESERT RHINO CAMP

● Spot rare desert-adapted wildlife during daily game drives ● Join expert black rhino trackers on foot ● Support locals and the Save the Rhino Trust simply by staying here

If helping to protect an endangered species while exploring one of the most rugged and remote landscapes on the planet (in style) sounds like your cup of tea, then leading luxury sustainable safari operator Wilderness Safaris has the escape for you.

Nestled in the heart of Namibia's massive Palmwag Concession, home to the largest free-ranging population of black rhinoceros in all of Africa, Desert Rhino Camp's mission is to assist in the conservation of the desert-adapted rhino species, whose populations are finally on the rebound after facing near-extinction at the hands of illegal poachers. The ultra-low-impact camp, one of seven run by Wilderness Safaris in Namibia, is operated in conjunction with local communities and Save the Rhino Trust, a non-profit committed to the cause. The species' remarkable comeback can largely be attributed to the efforts of the joint operation, with a portion of revenue reinvested into the trust.

Guests have the exclusive opportunity to join expert guides in tracking these magnificent giants on foot as part of the safari experience. Back at the camp, you'll be treated to gourmet Namibian fare highlighting local, seasonal ingredients, with evenings best spent swapping stories around a crackling bonfire beneath star-studded skies. Afterwards, retire to one of the eight elevated Meru-style canvas tents featuring energy-efficient lights and appliances, and hot water provided by solar-powered geysers.

ON YOUR DOORSTEP
The nearby freshwater spring also supports healthy populations of other desert-adapted wildlife, including lions, elephants, cheetahs, Hartmann's mountain zebras, leopard, giraffes, springboks and a prolific assortment of birdlife.

$ *Per night all-incl per person from ZAR5611*

🍽 *Gourmet Namibian-inspired fare*

☛ **Damaraland; www.wilderness-safaris.com. From Windhoek, the camp is around 2½ hours by car**

NEPAL

BARDIA ECOLODGE

● *Track Bengal tigers and greater one-horned rhinos on walking and jeep safaris*
● *Soak up the serenity of one of Nepal's lesser-visited national parks*

When it comes to wildlife-watching in Nepal, most travellers gravitate to Chitwan National Park, which is known for its robust population of greater one-horned rhino. But in the country's remote northwest, lesser-visited Bardia National Park isn't just a fantastic place to spot these incredible animals (away from the crowds), but here you're also more likely to lay eyes on an elusive Bengal tiger.

Of the string of budget tourist accommodations that fringe the national park, Bardia Ecolodge is a real find. Constructed with local materials and labour, the carbon-neutral lodge is solar-powered, plastics are minimised, and produce is grown or sourced locally. With mud walls and handmade bed quilts, rooms are simple but homely. Not that you'll have much time to get cosy, as your stay will be filled with outdoor adventures. While most visitors opt for at least one jeep safari (the lodge discourages elephant-back safaris), the most thrilling way to explore the jungle is on a walking safari with site manager and lifelong local Madhu, who knows the national park like the back of his hand. While tiger and rhino sightings are never guaranteed, there's plenty of other wildlife to be spotted, such as deer, otter, crocodiles, an array of birdlife, and maybe even a jungle cat. At the end of the day, a delicious healthy meal awaits

in the lodge dining area, which overlooks a crystal clear river bordering the park.

ON YOUR DOORSTEP
Take a stroll along the main road in a southerly direction from the lodge, which passes through a string of typical local villages that have helped to safeguard the resources and biodiversity of the national park by adopting sustainable agriculture methods.

$ *2-night stay incl meals, full-day walking safari and full-day jungle drive per person US$165*

🍴 *Healthy, hearty local and international fare*

☛ **Thakurdawa, Bardiya district; www.bardiaecolodge.com. It's a 50-minute flight or a 15-hour bus ride from Kathmandu to Nepalganj, from where a transfer can be arranged for the 3-hour drive to the lodge**

PANAMA

ISLAS SECAS

● *Discover pristine Panamanian dive sites* ● *Visit a penal colony turned marine reserve*
● *Spot more than 50 species of birds and an entire island dominated by a frigate colony*

Thirty kilometres off mainland Panama in the Gulf of Chiriquí, a veritable tropical Eden teems with life – and very little of it is human. Of the 14 islands that comprise the private Archipiélago de Islas Secas, only the largest is inhabited, and by a maximum of 18 guests at a time. It's peak low-impact luxury, with fully solar-powered operations, grey water irrigation, and food-scrap composting systems, among other initiatives.

By night, the pathways that connect Islas Secas' nine casitas to an open-air dining terraza and Hemingway-style lounge – which doubles as a mini museum for mysterious artefacts found on the island – dance with the scuttling of thousands of Halloween crabs. By day, the entire archipelago is up for discovery.

The abundant waters of the Gulf of Chiriquí offer some of the world's best fishing and diving. Regardless of skill level, guests can scuba or snorkel with critically endangered sea turtles (including olive ridley and loggerhead), brilliantly coloured parrotfish, and harmless whitetip sharks cutting through the currents. On land, birders go bonkers for Islas Cavada and Coco, home to more than 50 species of migratory birds and Panama's second largest colony of frigates, respectively. When exhaustion hits, Isla Pargo's virgin white sand beach, without a footprint on its shore, is primed for a relaxing afternoon lunch and Champagne picnic.

Well worth the additional cost, an adventurous, full-day excursion to Unesco-listed Coiba National Park reveals one of the world's largest protected marine areas and the second largest coral reef in the Eastern Pacific. Isla Coiba, the biggest of the 38 islands in the park, was home to a penal colony for nearly a century, and left behind ample chilling tales of escaped inmates when it shuttered just 15 years ago.

$ *3-night stay for 2 all-incl US$4500*

🍽 *Gourmet Panamanian fusion with freshly caught seafood*

☞ *Archipiélago de Islas Secas; www. islassecas.com. From David, road and boat transfers to Islas Secas are provided*

PERU

INKATERRA GUIDE FIELDS STATION

● *Ride horses among rhinos while staying at a cattle ranch-turned-eco-camp* ● *Help preserve at-risk wildlife, support local communities and fight deforestation* ● *Look out for toucans and elusive jaguars*

Inkaterra has been blazing the trail for Peruvian ecotourism for more than 40 years, with a string of eco-luxe properties across the country. But now they have a wallet-friendly Amazon alternative: their base for researchers, scientists and conservation volunteers, which is also a former training facility for naturalist guides, has opened to paying guests.

Set close to the banks of the Madre de Dios River, just north of the Tambopata National Reserve in southeastern Peru, the wooden, thatched-roof cabañas-on-stilts – divided into two rooms with beds wrapped in a netting cocoon – and two pavilions holding 16 in four shared rooms, are clustered together in a clearing. And all are surrounded by a jungle soundtrack – the oropendola's chortle, the chatter of night monkeys and the constant hum of cicadas.

The main house is at the heart of the field station, the place for convivial, communal meals – organic chicken, river fish, fresh fruit plucked from the station's own model farm and bio orchard – where guests and guides get together and plan the next day's excursions.

Head out on day and night forest hikes with expert guides, take a boat across a mirror-flat oxbow lake, get a birds-eye view of the forest from a walkway strung above the jungle canopy and go caiman

$ *Shared room per person US$80*

....

|●| *Peruvian dishes with produce from the lodge's bio-orchard and farm*

....

☛ **Madre de Dios River, Maldonado; www.inkaterra. com. From Puerto Maldonado, Inkaterra will transfer you by boat to the lodge**

spotting on the moonlit river. Or check out the agronomy projects and palmetum.

Your stay supports the Inkaterra Asociación, Inkaterra's NGO, which undertakes scientific research for conservation, education and the wellbeing of local communities around numerous ecosystems in Peru. To date in the Madre de Dios river basin, it has protected 150 sq km of rainforest basin and slowed deforestation, as well as monitoring at-risk wildlife numbers and helping communities maintain traditional forest ways.

RUSSIA

LEAPRUS 3912

● *Explore the Elbrus area from the world's highest low-impact lodge* ● *Summit Mt Elbrus during the summer months* ● *Hit the slopes at nearby ski resorts*

Imagine you're high in Russia's Caucasus Mountains, with nothing but snowy peaks on the horizon. Suddenly, you come upon a wintry mirage: an otherworldly series of buildings that look like a cross between a space station and a Bond villain's secret lair.

But you're not seeing things. You've made it to the feat of high-altitude sustainable hotel design known as the LEAPrus 3912

hotel. Perched at 3912m in the foothills of Mt Elbrus, it's the world's highest hotel next to the teahouses in the upper reaches of Nepal's Everest Base Camp trail – with decidedly more creature comforts. Consisting of tube-like buildings raised to create a minimally invasive footprint, each lodging unit holds 12 bunk-style beds, with the best views realised from the floor-to-ceiling window in the communal dining and relaxing area. And don't let the word 'bunk' scare you off: this is as haute as high-altitude hostels get, with heated floors, high-tech heat retention, and fresh water sourced from snowmelt. LEAPrus is also off-the-grid, thanks to photovoltaic cells that generate the hotel's electricity, though, unbelievably, wi-fi is available.

There's plenty to do if you're a skier or mountaineer, but even if you're not, it's worth the trip to spend a night enjoying a glass of wine as the sun sets over the remote alpine landscape. Blankets and linens are provided, but you'll need to bring warm clothes for sleeping and exploring, as much of the region is snow-covered year-round.

ON YOUR DOORSTEP
Book your stay in June, July or August if you're hoping to reach Mt Elbrus' summit (5642m) on foot. While hiking boots are fine for lower elevations, you'll need expedition gear to complete the trek.

$ *Dorm bed per night incl meals (bookable via elbrusadventures. ru) from ₽6500*

🍴 *Communal, international buffet meals*

☛ *Terskol, Russia; http://leaprus.com. From Mineralnye Vody, most people make the 3-hour journey south to Terskol by share-taxi. From Terskol, it's a 30-minute drive to the hotel*

SOLOMON ISLANDS
TETEPARE ISLAND ECOLODGE

● *Snorkel with dugongs feeding on offshore seagrass beds* ● *Hike to traditional kastom (custom) sites* ● *Help rangers monitor endangered leatherback turtles*

Cloaked in virgin rainforest and fringed with biodiverse reefs, Tetepare is the largest uninhabited tropical island in the southern hemisphere. It's also home to a leading conservation project and a locally owned and managed eco-lodge offering one of the most unique low-impact stays in the Solomon Islands.

Run by the Tetepare Descendants' Association (TDA), recognised as the island's owners, the lodge – which can accommodate up to 18 guests at one time – comprises a cluster of traditional Melanesian leaf houses set near a sparkling lagoon. With shared bathroom facilities and solar energy providing lighting only (hint: ensure your camera is charged in advance) it's a proper wilderness experience, but you'll want to stay here for at least five days to make the most of the activities available, from snorkelling atop pristine coral reefs to spotting some of the island's 74 bird species. You can also take a moonlight coconut crab walk, or perhaps a hike through the jungle to the remnants of an abandoned village that offers clues as to how its original inhabitants – which mysteriously abandoned the island in the 1860s – once lived. If your visit aligns with a turtle monitoring session, you can even give the rangers a hand. With every visit providing meaningful employment opportunities to locals while also helping to conserve the island's resources so they may sustain the community for generations to come, it's the ultimate sustainable castaway experience.

ON YOUR DOORSTEP
For an extra SBD$700, a visit can be arranged to a nearby island village. Not only do these tours offer a fascinating window into local life far from the tourist trail, but an opportunity to support the communities if you're interested in beautiful traditional wood carvings, woven mats, and other souvenirs.

$ *Per night incl meals and some activities per person SBD$600 plus one-off conservation fee SBD$120*

🍽 *Solomon Islands cuisine highlighting fresh seafood*

☛ **Western Province; www.tetepare.org. Guests must take a domestic flight from the capital Honiara to Munda, from where a boat transfer (1-2 hours) must be prearranged**

SOUTH AFRICA

SHAMWARI PRIVATE GAME RESERVE

● *Camp on a remote plateau and feast around the campfire* ● *Begin and end the day seeing the Big Five* ● *Visit rhino and big cat rehabilitation centres*

Around Addo Elephant National Park is one of South Africa's best-known clusters of exclusive private game reserves, and the 70 sq km Shamwari is perhaps the most venerable of the lot. The 30-year-old conservation project has animals from the Big Five to 275 bird species roaming five of South Africa's eight biomes, dominated by Albany thicket with its endemic puff adders, flightless dung beetles, Spekboom succulents and spike-thorn trees. As well as spotting towering giraffes, plenty of zebras and ambling elephants on wildlife drives and walks, guests can visit the Wildlife Rehabilitation Centre, which raises rhinos and other poaching orphans and releases them into safe environments. There's also the Born Free Big Cat Sanctuaries, caring for lions and other felines rescued from captivity, and responsible volunteering opportunities through the Shamwari Conservation Experience.

Accommodation options range from six luxurious safari lodges to the intrepid thrill of the Explorer Camp. Swapping four wheels for a walking safari, the Explorer Camp comprises three tents, an outdoor bathroom and a plunge pool on a plateau amid basalt and granite extrusions. Sindile, the new luxury tented camp, has nine secluded 'tents' that outdo most hotel rooms, each with a private deck, heated plunge pool and indoor fireplace. Named

after a leopardess of local legend, the camp mimics a leopard's lair with its commanding views of the Bushman's River and plains. A Shamwari safari is an expensive, once-in-a-lifetime experience for most visitors, but the funds enable valuable conservation work.

ON YOUR DOORSTEP

Just 30km west, Addo Elephant National Park, South Africa's third-largest park at almost 2000 sq km, hosts not just the Big Five but the Big Seven (add great white sharks and southern right whales). Head to Grahamstown, 65km northeast, for history and a lively arts festival every July.

$ *Doubles all-incl per person from ZAR11,000*

••••••••••••••••••••••••••••••••••••

🍴 *Reinterpreted South African classics and haute lodge cuisine*

••••••••••••••••••••••••••••••••••••

☞ Paterson, Eastern Cape; www. shamwari.com. You can drive from Cape Town via the Garden Route by electric vehicle (820km), or hire a standard car from Port Elizabeth (80km)

SRI LANKA

GAL OYA LODGE

● *Spot elephants and more near your luxe jungle lodge* ● *Head out on hikes guided by naturalists or a local village chief* ● *Learn how to place and monitor wildlife-tracking cameras for research*

Sri Lanka has an impressive 26 national parks, but Gal Oya National Park, in the nation's southeast, is one of the least visited, which makes it the perfect location for a crowd-free jungle getaway. With only 10 rooms – all built with locally sourced materials – nestled between the foliage, Gal Oya Lodge gives you the feeling you're bedding down in the heart of the jungle – because you are. It's a true luxury to come back to your spacious bungalow after a sweaty hike, stand under the open-air rain shower, and watch the lizards and geckos scurry around on the foliage-covered stone walls. Mesh inserts between the ceiling and walls ensure the exotic critters stay out of your bedroom, though large mosquito nets are provided for good measure.

The same can't be said for the two-level lounge and dining room – but that's part of the luxury wilderness lodge's appeal. Because it's located in the park's buffer zone, wildlife is known to migrate through the common areas. Handily, Gal Oya has an on-site research centre used by in-house naturalists and partner organisations to

monitor the numbers and migration patterns of several of the park's endangered species, including leopards and elephants. During your stay, you can learn about and participate in projects with the resort's naturalists. One particularly interesting programme is a video monitoring study of fishing cats, a vulnerable species endemic to Southeast Asia.

ON YOUR DOORSTEP
Among the activities on offer at the lodge is the option to take a boat safari on Senanayake Samudraya Reservoir, one of Sri Lanka's largest lakes, during which you might be lucky enough to spot elephants swimming between its islands.

$ *Camping per night per person from KES1000 plus US$90 daily conservancy fee*

⦿ *Locally sourced international and Sri Lankan dishes*

☛ **Inginiyagalla Rd, Uva province; www.galoyalodge.com. Gal Oya Lodge is 3½ hours drive west of Kandy. The lodge can arrange transfers to and from Kandy, Ella, or Colombo**

SWEDEN

KOLARBYN ECOLODGE

● *Spot moose and beavers on guided hikes and paddles* ● *Learn how to forage for ingredients to cook yourself* ● *Rewild yourself while staying in a primitive forest hut*

Up until the 1950s, Sweden's forests were filled with primitive wooden huts built by forest workers who burned wood to make charcoal for the iron and steel industries. Fast forward to the 1990s, and a group of retired forest workers from the town of Skinnskatteberg were concerned this cultural heritage would be lost with the disintegrating huts and decided to build new ones in the local forest. A decade later, the 12 cosy, moss-covered huts opened for tourists as Kolarbyn: Sweden's most primitive (and arguably most sustainable) hotel.

Managed by Wild Sweden, visits to Kolarbyn are run as a three-night 'adventure', including guided forest hikes (look out for moose!), beaver-spotting boat trips in a nearby river, and optional wilderness survival training with local bushcraft expert Jonas Landolsi. Your guide will also show you how to forage for wild edibles to spice up your meals, with nature's supermarket supplemented by local produce such as wild boar and organic vegetables. To drink, there are beers from the local microbrewery, or drinking water collected from a local spring. After dinner, simply roll out your sleeping

$ *3-night adventures incl meals and activities SEK6,950*

●l *Cook your own meal over an open fire*

☛ **Skinnskatteberg, www.wildsweden. com. Kolarbyn is 2 hours' drive, or 3 hours by train, northwest of Stockholm**

bags in your hut, which, like the old days, is warmed by a wood-burning stove. There are no showers, but it wouldn't be Sweden without a sauna, and here it floats on the lake, where you can take a restorative plunge afterwards.

ON YOUR DOORSTEP
Kolarbyn is located on the edge of lake Skärsjön, with canoes available should you fancy a paddle. Alternatively, you can head out for solo hikes in the forest between guided activities.

TANZANIA
CHUMBE ISLAND CORAL PARK

● Observe the world's largest crabs roaming the island after dark ● Snorkel atop one of Africa's most dazzling coral reefs ● Support the conservation of threatened wildlife

A string of tropical islands just 35km off mainland Tanzania, Zanzibar is a popular spot to wind down after a safari holiday. Yet on a small coral atoll off the main island of Unguja, there's another incredible wildlife experience to be had.

Considered to be the world's first private marine protected area, Chumbe Island Coral Park encompasses a coral reef sanctuary, a forest reserve, a visitor centre, and a seven-room eco-lodge built with the aim of having no negative impact on the environment – right down to the homemade biodegradable soap and insect repellant.

Most people opt to visit the uninhabited island on a day trip from Unguja, which includes a snorkelling session on the house reef (home to more than 200 coral species and 440 identified fish species), a forest walk (look out for the rare Aders' duiker), climbing the island's historic lighthouse for magical views of the island, and a delicious lunch. But arguably the best experience can only be had after dark, when the island's 300-odd coconut (also known as robber) crabs come out to feed on anything they can get their claws on. Weighing up to 4kg, it's easy to understand why these enormous crustaceans are now thought to be extinct on Unguja, where around a third of the population lives below the poverty line.

With tourism helping to fund Chumbe's environmental awareness programme, which provides free enviro-education to schools, fishers, community groups and government officials, you can sleep easy in your loft-style hut, which looks out over the turquoise sea. If you've brought your own snorkel mask, consider donating it to the island, which is visited by 500 local students every year.

$ *Doubles all-incl per person US$260*

🍽 *Locally caught seafood and Zanzibarian curries*

☛ **Chumbe Island, Zanzibar; www.chumbeisland.com. Boat transfers (30 minutes) arrive and depart from Mbweni Ruins Hotel, a 10-minute taxi ride south of Stone Town**

TANZANIA

ABALI RIDGE

● Explore one of Africa's most remote and beautiful parks ● Spot big cats, elephants and rare antelopes with expert guides on game drives and bush walks ● Help fund the Ruaha Carnivore Project

The opening of Asilia's Jabali Ridge in 2017 put the wild and beautiful Ruaha National Park – one of Africa's best-kept secrets – well and truly on the safari map.

The architecture is as stunning as the setting: built on a hill overlooking a forest of ancient baobabs and boundless plains, it takes its cue from the landscape. Eight suites cocooned by colossal boulders are all sustainably sourced blonde wood and baobab-grey stone, with vast beds clad in hand-dyed linens and louvred wood shuttered walls that open on to a spacious terrace.

Ruaha is a place of ephemeral sand rivers, granite kopjes and palm-studded plains but its remoteness means it gets a fraction of the Serengeti's visitors. It may be the size of a small country but with your hawk-eyed Asilia guide accompanying you on morning, afternoon and nocturnal game drives and bush walks, you won't miss a thing. Perhaps prides of lion – the park is home to a tenth of the world's population and Jabili donates to the pioneering Ruaha Carnivore Project – parades of elephants, dazzles of zebra and journeys of giraffe, even pangolin, that notoriously difficult-to-spot scaly mammal that tops every safari guides' bucket list.

Between exploring, flop into a hammock or take a dip in the infinity pool watched over by a host of cute and curious bush hyrax. Or head to the one-room spa where the 'African wood massage' will pummel out any knots and shea butter will soothe sun-frazzled skin. Then enjoy a fine South African wine or craft gin before dining in the open-fronted restaurant under a star-studded sky, as hyenas whoop and lions roar into the night.

$ *Doubles all-incl from US$1640*

....

🍴 *Gourmet international cuisine*

....

☛ **Ruaha National Park, Iringa; www. asiliaafrica.com. From Dar es Salaam, it's a 10-hour drive or a 2½-hour scheduled or charter flight to Ruaha's airstrip**

UGANDA
VOLCANOES SAFARIS

● *View endangered gorillas and chimpanzees in their natural habitat*
● *Track primates on foot* ● *Directly fund community-led conservation projects*

At the forefront of reviving wildlife tourism in Rwanda and Uganda since 1997, Volcanoes Safaris was the first company of its kind to offer luxury lodge-based accommodations and mountain gorilla and chimpanzee tracking experiences in East Africa. It's a tourism model built to both protect and preserve the region's impressive wildlife and local cultures. Guests can visit Volcanoes Safaris' three lodges in Uganda (and one in Rwanda) individually or book a multi-lodge safari journey to discover the region in more depth, with US$100 from each booking directly benefiting the Volcanoes Safaris Partnership Trust, a non-profit that supports local communities and conservation activities near each lodge.

At Mount Gahinga Lodge in Uganda, nestled at the base of the Virunga Volcanoes next to Mgahinga Gorilla National Park, guests can stay in luxury *bandas* (stone huts with papyrus roofs) and partake in mountain gorilla or golden monkey tracking experiences. Overlooking the primeval Bwindi Impenetrable Forest, Volcanoes Bwindi Lodge in Uganda envelopes guests in an ethereal jungle canopy within easy distance of trekking with gorillas, while at the eclectic and contemporary Kyambura Gorge Lodge on the edge of Uganda's Queen Elizabeth National Park, you can track chimpanzees in a sunken forest. Extend your trip into Rwanda at Virunga

Lodge, a 10-*banda* property perched on a ridge with views of the Virunga Volcanoes and the Musanze valley and an ideal base to track the country's endangered mountain gorillas.

ON YOUR DOORSTEP

Travellers can visit and support myriad social projects near each hotel, including Bwindi Bar near Bwindi Lodge, a community restaurant and training institution, and a women's coffee cooperative near Kyambura Gorge Lodge.

$ *Doubles from US$315*

◉| *International cuisine with East African flair*

☛ *Lodges in Rwanda and Uganda; www.volcanoessafaris.com*

USA
ROAM BEYOND KALALOCH

- ● *Hike with Roosevelt elk at the gateway to the Unesco-listed Olympic National Park*
- ● *Explore the Olympic Peninsula coast on the doorstep of your comfy off-grid 'glamper'*

A sort of micro-community in the middle of nowhere, Roam Beyond's collection of mobile dwellings gives exclusive access to the Olympic Peninsula's unparalleled wilderness without disrupting it. Decked out with hammocks, communal tables, a covered lounge area, and lawn games like bocce and cornhole, the site features fully off-grid, portable cabin-like pods powered by the sun and built with responsibly sourced materials, sans plastic finishes, and with wool insulation.

Both the Unesco-listed Olympic National Park and Hoh Rain Forest are at your doorstep, as is the coast, meaning near-limitless hiking and more animals than people in residence – look for Roosevelt elk in the forest. Thousands of old-growth logs on the beach, a mere stumble from the site, are perfect to perch upon and toast the sun as it sets over the water, rippling with humpback whales and sea otters.

ON YOUR DOORSTEP
An easy 5km hike north ends at Kalaloch Lodge, where you can refuel with a hot meal and a stiff drink. Restock basic supplies at Queets Trading Post, a small convenience store a 10-minute drive southeast.

$ *2-night stay for up to four US$520; available May to October*

🍽 *Cook your own dinner over the firepit*

☛ *Kalaloch, WA; www.roambeyond. travel/kalaloch. Public transport from Seattle is feasible, or it's a 3-hour drive*

- Eco-luxury
- Sustainable Dining
- Wellness

RELAXATION

ARUBA

Bucuti & Tara Beach Resort

● *Stay at a seaside resort paving an eco-trail in the Caribbean* ● *Head to the Puran Spa for a facial with locally grown aloe* ● *Take a therapeutic painting class or attend a smoothie 'wellness hour'*

Bucati & Tara Beach Resort is a real-world example of how luxury and sustainability need not be mutually exclusive. From the large infinity pool to sunset hours set to the soundtrack of a local steel-drum band, it's got all the makings of a great hotel. What makes it different from most adults-only beach resorts, however, is that it practices sustainable luxury, and that means more than just serving fair-trade coffee. Thanks to its extensive solar system, on-site water filtration plant, and use of local products, the resort is the first in the Caribbean to be completely carbon-neutral. Community initiatives include student sustainability tours, beach clean-ups for guests and staff, and an animal rescue programme in which Bucuti & Tara covers the cost of veterinary services and paperwork for guests keen to adopt a rescue animal from the island.

ON YOUR DOORSTEP

Urvin Croes, the local chef behind buzzed-about Aruba restaurants White Modern and The Kitchen Table works closely with island farmers and the local culinary school to create low-impact dishes that tell a story about the history and culture of the Caribbean.

$ *Doubles from US$583*

🍽 *International*

☛ *L.G Smith Blvd 55B, Oranjestad; www.bucuti.com*

AUSTRALIA
LONGITUDE 131°

● *Gaze at Uluru from your luxury glamping tent* ● *Indulge in a spa treatment with a healing balm made by local Aboriginal women* ● *Feast on some of Australia's best native produce*

Nothing can prepare you for the immensity, grandeur, and stillness of Uluru. And while Australia's most famous rock looks incredible from any angle, it's difficult to beat admiring its mesmerising colour transformation throughout the day from your luxury tented room at Longitude 131°.

Constructed in line with some of Australia's strictest environmental and cultural regulations, the resort's 16 tented pavilions – furnished with every low-impact amenity you could want – are designed to 'float' above the ancient sand dunes southeast of Yulara, Uluru's tourism hub. But its sustainability cred doesn't end there. Part of the boutique Baillie Lodges group, a collection of ultra-sustainable luxury lodges in unique Australian wilderness destinations, Longitude 131° harnesses much of its power from solar, has showers instead of baths in the rooms to preserve water, pumps waste out to Yulara, and grows a selection of fresh produce (with food waste used as compost) to further reduce its carbon footprint. The lodge also works closely with the local Aboriginal community, which led to the launch of an artist-in-residence programme in 2019 that allows guests the opportunity to chat with artists while they create their works in the resort's central Dune House.

Reopened in 2017 following an extensive refurbishment, Longitude 131° isn't only looking snazzier than ever, but with climbing Uluru banned in 2019, the views have arguably never been better.

ON YOUR DOORSTEP
Rates include essential Uluru experiences such as sunset viewing and walks around Uluru and nearby Kata Tjuta, but bespoke experiences – such as a tour of the remote Ernabella Arts Studio, Australia's oldest continuously running indigenous arts centre, allow you to engage more deeply with local culture.

$ *2-night stay all-incl per person from AU$3200*

....

●| *Fine modern Australian dining*

....

☞ **Yulara, Northern Territory; www. longitude131.com.au**

BOLIVIA
KACHI LODGE

● Explore Uyuni's otherworldly mystique from a sustainable-luxe base ● Head out on hikes guided by naturalists or a local village chief ● Sip Singani cocktails above the salt flats

For nature lovers and thrill seekers across the globe, the Uyuni Salt Flats in Bolivia have long-ranked atop the world's must-visit extreme destinations. Following the 2019 opening of Kachi Lodge, there's now a new way to discover this otherworldly escape in eco-luxury.

Sitting on Bolivia's Altiplano at a cool 3597m, this posh lodge at the foot of the Tunupa volcano evokes a futuristic space station. Overlooking the largest salt flats on earth, the orb-shaped domes offer panoramic views of the star-studded sky and dramatic landscapes. Inside, the minimalist domes are decorated with a series of artworks inspired by the local Andean culture and created by Gaston Ugalde, Bolivia's most celebrated contemporary artist. The menu also reflects thoughtful Bolivian influence, and everything served at Kachi Lodge is exclusively locally sourced. At Gustu Restaurant, guests can sample llama tartar while sipping a cocktail made with Singani, the country's flagship spirit – just don't expect a disposable straw, because a strict zero-plastic policy is enforced throughout.

Built upon a wooden floor to avoid damaging the salt crust, the solar-powered lodge (which is fully mobile) employs a state-of-the-art water treatment system that recycles itself in a closed loop, meaning no waste is pumped into the landscape. Outside, heart-racing activities include downhill mountain biking, trekking to the volcano's crater and hiking to the top of Kachi Island to witness one of South America's most breathtaking sunsets.

ON YOUR DOORSTEP
The colonial constructions of Coquesa, the archaeological site of Alcaya and an antique train cemetery are all a short drive from the lodge. From December to March, guests can also paddleboard across the natural mirror created by the flooded salt flats.

$ *2-night stay all-incl per person from USD$1980*

🍽 *Locally sourced, authentic Bolivian cuisine*

☛ **Uyuni Salt Flats, Bolivia; www. kachilodge.com. Rates include transfers from Uyuni to the lodge (98km)**

CANADA

FOGO ISLAND INN

● *Step out into nature from an architecturally stunning, low-impact base* ● *Soak away your worries in the rooftop hot tub* ● *Feast on fresh crab, shrimp and cod*

A stay at Fogo Island Inn, on the northeast coast of Newfoundland, is all about immersing yourself in and connecting with the tranquility of the wild. A gateway to explore the Labrador Strait's famous Iceberg Alley, this remote retreat is set on the largest island in a 100-island archipelago at the eastern edge of the North American continent and is perched on stilts for minimal environmental impact on the area's rocks, lichens, and berries, equipping each of the 29 guest rooms with boundless views of the sea and sky.

Founded by Canadian entrepreneur and Fogo Island local Zita Cobb to promote cultural and economic resiliency for her hometown, the hotel's profits are reinvested into the community, which is actively involved in the guest experience. With community hosts as guides, guests can enjoy a range of excursions: exploring the island's 200km of ancient footpaths, setting sail off the wild Atlantic coast with a crab fisher, or learning how to make jams and jellies from wild partridgeberries and blueberries with an expert forager.

Back on property, you can cosy up beside one of six wood-burning fireplaces and work your way through the inn's extensive literature collection, take in a film at the in-house cinema, relax in the rooftop spa with hot tubs and a sauna, and linger over delicious meals at the restaurant with floor-to-ceiling views of the Atlantic.

ON YOUR DOORSTEP

The lodge is an ideal base to visit all four contemporary art locations of Fogo Island Arts Studios designed by Todd Saunders, a native of Gander who built the off-grid studios with compost toilets, solar-powered energy, and wood-burning stoves.

$ *2-night stay for two all-incl CAD$3950*

🍽 *Contemporary Canadian, starring locally fished, farmed and foraged ingredients*

☛ *210 Main Rd, Joe Batt's Arm, Fogo Island, Newfoundland; www.fogoislandinn. ca. Transfers to the lodge can be arranged through the inn, including a land-and-ferry option*

CHILE

TIERRA ATACAMA

● *Take in an incredible Andes sunset by the infinity pool* ● *Sample natural Chilean products at the Uma Spa* ● *Enjoy meals with produce from the off-grid garden*

The driest non-polar place on Earth mightn't sound like the most sustainable place to build a luxury hotel, but Tierra Atacama is among the few hotels in the adventure hub of San Pedro de Atacama that have nailed it. Built inside the clay walls of a centuries-old cattle corral on the outskirts of town, the luxe hotel was the first in South America to become 100% solar-powered. But that's far from where its sustainability cred ends.

Featuring incredible views towards the Licanabur Volcano, the modern glass and adobe hotel – built with local materials – seamlessly blends into the desert landscape. Furnished with local textiles, its 32 spacious rooms offer eco-friendly amenities provided in reusable dispensers; even the sewing kits are plastic-free. Tierra Atacama also relies on its own well for water (a particularly valuable resource in San Pedro) and uses a reverse osmosis system to supply drinking water. Grey water is used to irrigate the lush gardens that supply the buffet restaurant, and its plastic-free philosophy extends to the containers used for food served on excursions, including a hike through otherworldly Moon Valley.

Your stay also helps to benefit the local community, with more than 40 students from the local Likan Antai technical school taken on as apprentices by the hotel to date, with some graduates going on to secure permanent roles.

ON YOUR DOORSTEP
In 2019 the hotel teamed with Chile's Foundation for Heritage Conservation to launch Ancestral Excursions based on the agriculture, food, crafts, architecture and cultural heritage of Atacama Desert people, offering an incredible opportunity to deepen your connection with local culture.

$ *2 nights all-incl per person from US$1400*

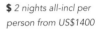 *Light, north Chilean cuisine with a modern twist*

☛ **Domingo Atienza, San Pedro de Atacama; www. tierrahotels.com. Rates include transfers from Calama, 75 minutes' drive west of the hotel**

COLOMBIA
Cannúa

● *Stay in a luxe cabana perched above the Colombian forest* ● *Start the day with coffee grown on a nearby organic farm* ● *Indulge in all-natural spa treatments*

Tucked in the verdant Valle de San Nicolas in the Central Andes, Cannúa revolutionised luxury eco-tourism in Colombia when it debuted in 2019 as the ultimate base for hikes along pre-Hispanic heritage trails, birdwatching expeditions, and visits to organic coffee and flower farms. Set within 27 acres of a protected forest and surrounded by traditional Antioquian fincas, this boutique retreat's 10-rooms and eight hexagonal private cabanas – some with private gardens and balconies – were built from sustainably sourced bamboo and compressed earth blocks produced on-site.

In line with Cannúa's holistic approach to sustainability in the Colombian countryside, guests can immerse in regenerative agriculture principles during guided walks in the property's organic gardens and 'food forest', which provide organic fare for Cannúa's cafe and restaurant. There's also a spa using products made from homegrown natural products.

ON YOUR DOORSTEP

Just 45 minutes' drive northwest from Cannúa is Arví Park, a 162-sq-km nature preserve and pre-Hispanic archeological site with nearly 50km of hiking trails and a cable car which connects to Medellín's metro system.

$ *Doubles from US$200*

🍽 *Colombian cuisine*

☞ ***Domingo Atienza, San Pedro de Atacama; www. tierrahotels.com. Cannúa can arrange transfers from Medellín***

COOK ISLANDS
IKURANGI ECO RETREAT

● *Bed down in the Cook Islands' only eco-glamping accommodation* ● *Start the day with a gourmet breakfast showcasing local fruits* ● *Book a yoga class on your private deck*

As one of the most popular honeymoon destinations in the South Pacific, the Cook Islands aren't short of luxury hotels. When it comes to character and sustainability, however, Ikuranji comes out on top. Tucked away behind the beach on the east coast of Rarotonga, Ikuranji offers a collection of stylishly appointed

glamping tents and one-bedroom *ares* (Polynesian for 'homes') designed to operate as sustainably as possible, from the design that promotes natural ventilation (negating the need for air-con) to the chemical-free plant-based bathroom amenities. Deeply rooted in the local community, the retreat is supplied by local artisans, actively supports and sponsors non-profit activities around the island, and pledges 5% of profits to conservation activities.

Set in a lush garden (irrigated by wastewater) with views towards the mountains of Takitumu, Ikuranji is a peaceful spot to kick back with a craft beer from the nearby Matutu Brewing Company or indulge in a massage or private yoga class, but the free bicycles on offer encourage guests to explore the local beaches and eat at local markets and restaurants. Should you prefer to eat in, a private chef can be arranged to prepare a gourmet island meal on your deck. The retreat's new owners, who took over in 2019, also plan to build an all-weather platform that can be used for yoga classes and group dining.

ON YOUR DOORSTEP
For an authentic taste of the Cook Islands, schedule a Saturday lunch stop at the local Punanga Nui Market. The nearby Muri Night Markets are also open several nights each week for dinner.

$ *3-night stay for 2 from NZD$299*

....

🍽 *Healthy tropical breakfast*

....

☛ **Address: Titami Rd, Matavera, Rarotonga; www. ikurangi.com.**

COSTA RICA

LAPA RIOS LODGE

● *Stay in a thatched-roof bungalow above the sea* ● *Savour responsibly caught seafood and organic South American wine* ● *Practise yoga in a relaxed jungle setting*

After serving as Peace Corps volunteers in Kenya in the late 1960s, US couple John and Karen Lewis moved to Costa Rica in the 1980s with the desire to preserve and sustain the country's rural communities. Being avid birdwatchers, they headed to the Osa Peninsula in southern Costa Rica with one mission: to prove that a rainforest left standing is worth more than one cut down. Setting the standard for ecotourism in the country, the couple's ambitious tourism project now protects 1000 verdant acres of Central America's last remaining lowland tropical rainforest.

Set adjacent to Corcovado National Park – where endangered pumas and jaguars roam the jungle floor and scarlet macaws circle above the treetops – the lodge encourages guests to explore the idyllic natural setting on guided nature walks and hikes, birdwatching expeditions, wildlife cruises, and reforestation expeditions where guests can plant trees in the wild.

After a day of adventures, kick back in one of 17 open-air, thatched-roof bungalows, all equipped with large hammocks, private verandas with outdoor showers, and views over a serene headland where the Golfo Dulce meets the wild Pacific Ocean's rare tropical fjords and cerulean tidepools. Enjoy the sprawling coastline's secluded beaches or the lodge's myriad amenities, from the saltwater pool to yoga classes, and tuck into fresh, healthy meals at Brisa Azul, the lodge's main restaurant.

ON YOUR DOORSTEP
Nearly 80% of the Osa Peninsula is protected, and guests can easily access Corcovado National Park, the lodge's neighbour, to spot endangered pumas and jaguars among ancient trees in one of Costa Rica's most biodiverse park systems.

$ *Doubles all-incl from US$595*

....

🍽 *Traditional Costa Rican and international cuisine*

....

☞ **Puerto Jiménez, Puntarenas province; www.laparios.com.**

CYPRUS
Amavi Hotel

● *Indulge at the spa using natural products without parabens, microbeads and other nasties*
● *Soak up the seafront location in suites using automation technology to minimise energy waste*

Recognising the need to balance tourism with environmental preservation, the Amavi Hotel is taking steps to become the first hotel in Cyprus to achieve the EU Ecolabel accreditation. It's also making a difference in the community. In 2011, it founded the Ithaki Association for the prevention and treatment of dementia in the local area. And Amavi is now on a mission to expand its facilities and services so they're available across the island.

Relaxation is at the heart of the hotel experience. It's an adults-only retreat on a Blue Flag beach, with a spa supported by Natural Spa Factory. Products take inspiration from the seasons and are free from chemicals and preservatives, including parabens, SLS and MCI, and microbeads. The frothy outdoor spa pool even includes poolside service: think eco aspirations with a touch of luxury.

ON YOUR DOORSTEP

In southwest Cyprus, Amavi is at the sweet spot between the beach bars and restaurants of Katos Pafos, and the cultural relics of ancient Pafos. It's a 20-minute walk from the Pafos Archeological Site, founded in the 4th century BC.

$ *3-night stay for 2 half-board from €432*

🍴 *Cypriot/Fusion*

☛ **Poseidonos Ave 22, Pafos; www. amavihotel.com**

DOMINICA

Secret Bay

● *Hunt invasive lionfish for your own supper* ● *Disconnect to reconnect where the rainforest meets the sea* ● *Stay in a low-impact cliffside villa above an intimate beach*

Dominica has earned the nickname Nature Island for its verdant, mountainous terrain, with as many rivers as there are days in the year. In the wake of 2017's Hurricane Maria, Secret Bay is one of the island's comeback stories. The intimate eco-luxury retreat, perched on a cliff above the sea, partially reopened in late 2018 with six villas and a newly added wellness pavilion and fine-dining restaurant showcasing indigenous herbs grown on-site. Meticulous care was taken to develop the site without heavy machinery, with vetiver grass planted to fortify the cliff for decades to come.

Intimacy and mindfulness are at the forefront here. Each decked-out villa has a full kitchen, private plunge pool, deck, and privacy provided by Mother Nature. Sure, there are plenty of activities — everything from yoga and sea cave exploring to private art lessons with a local artist — but the real treat here is being lulled away from the habit of 'doing' in favour of simply 'being.'

That being said, there are some not-to-be-missed experiences. Guests can venture to Prince Rupert Bay with a local fisher to learn how to hunt lionfish, an invasive (and delicious) species that threatens local biodiversity. After diving in to practise throwing spears at the bay's sandy floor, it's time to aim for the beautifully striped lionfish themselves. Whatever is caught comes back to shore for a beachside BBQ.

ON YOUR DOORSTEP

There are more than 5 sq km of protected wetlands, coral reefs, and tropical forests to explore at Cabrits National Park, just 15 minutes' drive north. Find local produce, spices, and more at the Portsmouth Saturday Market.

$ *3-night stay for 2 US$2956*

🍽 *Sustainable seafood, locally sourced*

☛ *Tibay, Portsmouth; www.secretbay.dm. Ferries to Dominica from neighbouring islands operate most days*

EL SALVADOR

PALO VERDE HOTEL

● Sip a fresh juice in the infinity pool while watching surfers ● Learn to surf just steps from your hotel room ● Feast on seafood fresh from La Libertad pier daily

Opened in 2017 by Camilo Menéndez, who grew up surfing El Salvador's waves, waterfront boutique hotel Palo Verde is a model for responsible tourism-based economic development in El Salvador. Beyond simply engaging small businesses and employing locals, Palo Verde offers employees a scholarship program, wherein they learn English and other tools to help them succeed in hospitality and break away from the gang violence that threatens many of their peers. In short, Palo Verde brings money that isn't from El Salvador into the community – and keeps that money there.

It also keeps guests from needing to leave, whether the goal is to chill, learn to surf, or study *español* at the in-house Spanish school. The property itself is stunningly minimalist: 10 open-layout rooms feature reclaimed wood, locally made linens, and rainwater showers. The on-site

restaurant, Olar de Mar, favours ingredients so fresh they don't need fussy foams to hide behind, and the included breakfast can't be skipped.

Sea caves are a short walk to the east, the town's longest beach to the west, and the hotel's crown jewel directly in front: Playa El Zonte's main point break, ideal for beginners and not far from the world-class Punta Roca break. You might even find Menéndez and his surfer buddies hanging by the infinity pool or checking conditions from the restaurant's deck. Rent yourself a board on-site, or book a lesson with International Surfing Association-certified Surfero's Surf School directly through Palo Verde.

ON YOUR DOORSTEP
A few minutes down the road, the port city of La Libertad has more life than El Zonte, including a fish market and places to try Salvadoran *horchata*, a milky refreshment spiced with cinnamon that's very different from its Mexican counterpart.

$ *Doubles US$129*

🍴 *Salvadoran fusion*

☛ **Km53 Carretera Litoral, Playa El Zonte, La Libertad, Chiltiupán; www. paloverdehotel.com**

ESTONIA

Projekt Kodu Retreat & Eco-Hostel

● *Soak in a unique outdoor mineral bath* ● *Embrace off-the-grid glamping in an Estonian national park* ● *Forage ingredients for your supper from the surrounding forest*

Known as the 'Land of Bays', Estonia's largest national park encompasses a 725 sq km swathe of coastline east of Tallinn. Crisscrossed with a network of hiking and biking trails, Lahemaa National Park is also home to Eastern Europe's coolest eco-camp.

Less than 10 minutes' drive south of Loksa, the park's main town, Projekt Kodu (kodu means 'home') invites guests to embrace off-the-grid glamping in characterful bell tents (including a shared dorm tent) furnished with plush ecologically washed linens and freshly picked wildflowers. Built with natural and reclaimed materials and designed to create the smallest environmental impact possible, the forest camp is powered by solar, and sources water from its own well. But while it's definitely rustic, its self-sustaining philosophy affords a few luxuries. Featuring homemade muesli and eggs from the camp's 'happy hens', the included breakfast is a real treat, as are the wholesome homemade vegetarian dinners that showcase homegrown, local and foraged produce (though you're welcome to cook your own foraged finds in the outdoor kitchen). Projekt Kodu's star feature, however, is its unique forest spa. After a long day exploring the national park, guests can relax in one of four outdoor (clothing optional) mineral baths, soak in the barrel hot tub, sweat it out in the sauna (all heated

$ *2-night stay for two from €176*

🍽 *Wholesome vegetarian meals featuring foraged ingredients*

☛ *Lahemaa National Park, Harju county; www.projekt-kodu. ee. Bus 155E runs from Tallinn to Loksa (about 90 minutes), from where the retreat will pick you up for the remaining 5km journey*

with straw bales or wood), or take a dip in the plunge pool. There's also complimentary twice-daily yoga, an outdoor fireplace, and water beds for stargazing in the forest!

ON YOUR DOORSTEP
Rent a bike for the 1km cycle to Hara beach for sunset. Prefer exploring on foot? The 7km Majakiyi Nature Trail weaves through lush forest and marshland, and takes in Lahemaa's largest erratic boulder.

FIJI

MAQAI BEACH ECO RESORT

● *Join locals in preparing a traditional lovo feast with locally grown and raised produce*
● *Treat yourself to a relaxing coconut back massage after a day out surfing*

Fiji is home to some of the best beach resorts in the South Pacific, and while many have made great strides towards sustainability in recent years, Maqai Beach was founded on its principles. Set up by an intrepid bunch of surfers in 2009, Maqai might not be Fiji's most luxurious resort, but for what it lacks in bells and whistles, this cute surf camp in the country's remote north makes up for in its low-impact mission.

Built from local and recycled materials, the solar-powered resort has implemented comprehensive waste management measures, and funnels profits back into the resort and community projects. Gifted a 10% stake in Maqai, the neighbouring village of Naivivi is heavily involved in resort life, with locals employed at all job levels, and lodge needs – from fresh fish to roof thatching – sourced as locally as possible. This close relationship immerses guests in Fijian culture.

When you're not out snorkelling, kayaking or surfing uncrowded nearby breaks, you can opt to visit the local village, take a guided jungle hike, or perhaps take part in a traditional kava ceremony. Once a week, guests are encouraged to get involved in the preparation of a traditional *lovo* feast (cooked in an underground fire pit). Other meals served at the beachfront Sandbar restaurant feature ingredients grown in the on-site organic garden, with fresh fish regularly on the menu. Better yet, food scraps are sent to the village to feed pigs, which are then purchased by the resort.

ON YOUR DOORSTEP
The resort also offers excursions to Bouma Heritage Park on neighbouring Taveuni island. Choose between a full-day walking or kayaking expedition to a set of twin waterfalls, or an easy trip to a series of three waterfalls known as the Tovoro Falls.

$ *Double bures from FJD$350 plus meals per person per day FJD$125*

🍽 *Organic Fijian fusion flavours*

☛ *Qamea Island; www.maqai.com*

FRENCH POLYNESIA

THE BRANDO

● *Stumble into the turquoise sea from your luxe beachfront villa built with local materials* ● *Feast on sustainably caught seafood* ● *Sign up for a holistic Polynesian treatment at the cocoon-like spa*

A quintessential tropical island escape fit for a Hollywood star, this magnificent resort redefined eco-luxury upon its 2014 opening. The concept dates back to the 1960s, when iconic US actor Marlon Brando purchased Teti'aroa with the vision to create a sustainable development that would resonate with visitors while providing meaningful opportunities to the people of French Polynesia. Today, the enchanting 35-villa property sprawls across a verdant atoll, featuring stunning vantage points, a world-class spa and three restaurants that showcase the bountiful produce grown on-island.

$ *2-night stay for two all-incl €6600*

....

🍽 *Polynesian-inspired fusion dishes and classic French cuisine*

....

☛ **Teti'aroa Private Island; www. thebrando.com**

Since its inception, the resort has implemented a series of innovative programmes and cutting-edge technologies to realise a goal of carbon neutrality. Energy demands, for example, have been reduced by nearly 70%, thanks to its groundbreaking seawater air-con system, which harnesses cold water from the depths of the ocean to produce a highly efficient cooling system for the buildings. Cycling is the preferred mode of transportation on the island, and most guests spend their days soaking up the dazzling setting by kayak, stand-up paddleboard, or snorkel. The resort also established the Tetiaroa Society, a non-profit designed to enhance the ecosystem and preserve local culture, ensuring a bright future for indigenous island communities. And while a visit to The Brando doesn't come cheap, at least it's a splurge travellers with deep enough pockets can justify.

ON YOUR DOORSTEP
Register for The Green Tour (one of the resort's most popular tours) which takes guests on a comprehensive journey to learn more about the Brando's sustainable facilities, including the 'eco-station', solar panels, coconut-oil powered electric plant, organic gardens, bee hives and more.

● **Sustainable Dining**   ● **Wellness**

THE GAMBIA
FOOTSTEPS ECO-LODGE

● *Learn to cook Gambian food with a local chef while staying at a community-minded beachside lodge* ● *Practise yoga in the resort's fruit tree gardens*

The Gambia is often overlooked during most people's Africa holiday planning, but the continent's smallest nation packs in much to do, from touring wildlife reserves to strolling rarely crowded beaches. More activities await at Footsteps Eco-Lodge, like boat safaris on a traditional wooden pirogue and guided photography tours. An especially memorable experience is the reptile tour in a nearby forest, though ophidiophobes may prefer to lounge by the resort's freshwater pool.

What will really make you fall in love with Footsteps is its dedication to community betterment. The resort was founded by an expat who realised the economic benefits of tourism weren't trickling down to workers. So at Footsteps, all staff have access to career training, paid time off, sick leave, and a comfortable living wage. Offerings of pesticide-free foods, natural air-con, and water recycling are just icing on the cake for eco-minded guests.

ON YOUR DOORSTEP
The Gambia has no shortage of adventure-focused activities, but if you're interested in Gambian languages and culture, spend the day collecting artefacts with the founder of the nearby Gunjur Village Museum (gunjurmuseum.com).

$ *Doubles from £40*

🍽 *Gambian and European; weekly buffets and BBQs*

☛ **Gunjur; www. footstepsin thegambia.com**

GREECE

MILIA MOUNTAIN RETREAT

● *Unwind and recharge in a laid-back preserved medieval village* ● *Immerse yourself in Mother Nature while hiking or cycling* ● *Enjoy Cretan hospitality and cook some local specialities.*

For nearly 30 years, Milia Mountain Retreat has been a beloved getaway for locals and international travellers alike. Perched high in the mountains of western Crete, the award-winning eco-lodge is completely off the grid and provides an idyllic setting for a romantic escape or digital detox.

Once a small but bustling medieval village, Milia was eventually abandoned and left to ruin. Luckily, a pair of local friends saw its potential after years of neglect, and decided to transform it into a sustainable retreat by restoring its deserted homes. Funded by a grant from the Greek government, they began the challenging restoration in 1990, working exclusively with local craftworkers who implemented time-honoured techniques and locally sourced materials to preserve the village's authentic charm. The project was completed with painstaking detail and took more than three years to finish, but the overall ecological footprint was almost zero. Today, it's considered a pristine example of local medieval architecture and a beacon of modern-day Cretan hospitality.

Electricity comes entirely from solar energy, water is sourced from the local spring, and during the winter months, heat is provided by wood-burning stoves and fireplaces. Guests are also welcome to learn local recipes during cooking classes held on-site each Wednesday, or join organised hiking tours every Friday to unwind in Crete's natural beauty. Simply by visiting, you can help to support the preservation of Crete's centuries-old heritage.

ON YOUR DOORSTEP

For some fresh air, cycle through town or hit one of the five popular hiking trails located just beyond the lodge's front door. The restaurant's gift shop has handmade souvenirs for sale.

$ *Doubles from €86*

....

🍽 *Creative Cretan cuisine highlighting seasonal homegrown produce*

....

☛ *Vlatos, Crete; www.milla.gr*

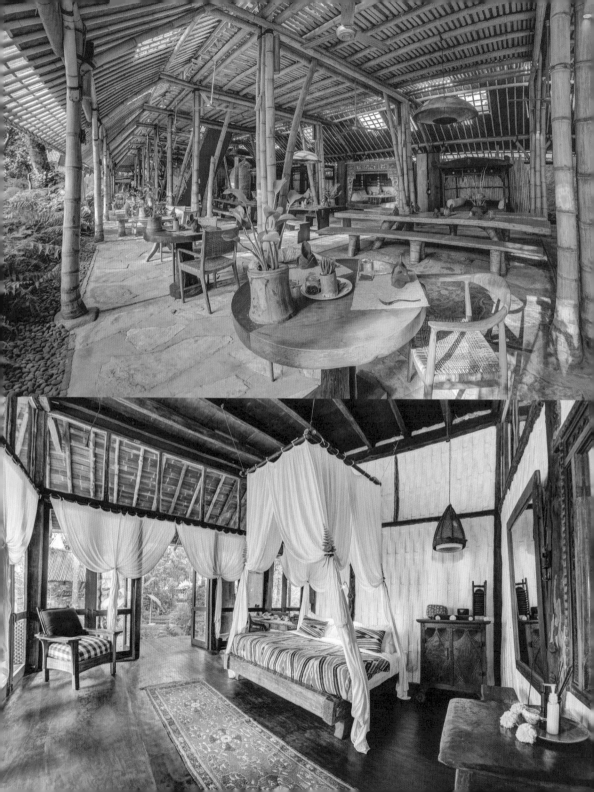

INDONESIA

BAMBU INDAH

● *Be at one with the jungle in a luxe bamboo tree house* ● *Eat delicious farm-to-table fare off banana-leaf plates* ● *Re-energise your travel-weary body in the bamboo massage pod*

Bali has long-struggled to sustainably manage the volume of tourists it receives, so if you're bent on visiting Indonesia's most famous holiday isle, it's all the more important to choose an ultra-low-impact sleep. Enter jewellery designers and long-term Bali residents John and Cynthia Hardy's sustainable masterpiece Bambu Indah. Originally a retreat for family and friends, the tranquil village-esque jungle resort on the outskirts of Ubud in the island's lush interior now invites mindful travellers to enjoy this eco-friendly slice of Balinese paradise.

Choose to stay in one of the 11 repurposed antique Javanese bridal homes, all exquisitely decorated with treasures found on the owners' travels, or in one of the awe-inspiring bamboo structures. Of particular note is the sweeping curves and hand-hammered copper bathtub of Cooper House and the 'floating' treetop tents (complete with giant retractable mosquito net domes) with knockout valley vistas.

A particularly valuable resource on Bali, water is treated with the utmost respect at Bambu Indah; guests are encouraged to reuse towels and linens and the all-natural organic bathroom amenities help to keep Bali's waterways clean. There's a swimming 'pond' fed by a stream that gurgles through the property, two on-site restaurants dish up delicious local cuisine crafted from produce grown on the property

or sourced locally, and in line with Bambu Indah's 'no plastics' policy, many of the tasty meals are served on banana-leaf plates.

ON YOUR DOORSTEP
Join a tour of nearby Bamboo U, part of Bambu Indah's Green Family of low-impact businesses, to learn about bamboo and its potential as the sustainable timber of the future. Choose from a one-day introduction or immerse yourself in a three- or 11-day experience.

$ *Doubles from US$110*

🍽 *Organic Balinese cuisine and healthy salads*

☛ *Jalan Baung Sayan, Ubud, Bali; www.bambuindah. com*

below & right: Bawah Reserve

INDONESIA

Bawah Reserve

● *Dine on fresh seafood in an atmospheric 'tree house'* ● *Luxuriate in an overwater villa constructed by hand* ● *Start the day with a Pilates class by the sea*

Ever loved a holiday spot so much you wished you could buy it? When Singapore-based entrepreneur Tim Hartnoll discovered a picturesque cluster of six islands in Indonesia's remote Anambas archipelago on a sailing trip, he did exactly that. And in 2018, he opened his own luxury hideaway on its largest isle.

Surrounded by turquoise lagoons, coral reefs and verdant jungle, Bawah is a suitably luxurious base for a relaxing break spent migrating between the island group's 13 beaches and the resort's four bars and restaurants. But what makes it really special is the legwork that went into ensuring that Bawah would have a minimal effect on its pristine location. Built over six years without heavy machinery, the resort was constructed primarily from bamboo, recycled teak and driftwood, allowing its 11 overwater bungalows, 21 beachfront suites and three garden suites to blend seamlessly into the island landscape. Seawater is desalinated for drinking, wastewater is treated on-site, power is largely generated by solar, and the resort even has a permaculture farm. Hartnoll also established the not-for-profit

$ 3-night stay for two, incl meals US$5940

....

🍽 *Mediterranean-inspired fine dining with a local twist*

....

☛ **Pulau Bawah, Anambas archipelago, Riau; www.bawahreserve. com**

Bawah Foundation upon the resort's opening to help conserve and expand the diversity of the Anambas Islands, as well as lift the welfare of its people. Bawah's owners also worked with the Indonesian government to see the area declared a nature reserve. Three are also complimentary daily spa treatments to consider while you're mulling over the price tag.

ON YOUR DOORSTEP
Download Bawah's snorkelling map and explore its pristine reefs at your leisure. You can also explore the small island group by kayak or stand-up paddleboard, or admire the reef more closely on a scuba-diving trip.

● **Eco-luxury**   ● **Sustainable Dining**   ● **Wellness**

INDONESIA
CEMPEDAK

● *Luxuriate in a naturally air-conditioned private-island villa* ● *Enjoy meals showcasing produce from a permaculture farm* ● *Experience pure island bliss from your massage bed overlooking the ocean*

Your first glimpse of the cresting wave-shaped villa roofs rising out of the jungle provides a hint that you've arrived somewhere special. But this adults-only private resort named for the island it sits on is more than just a luxury escape from Singapore.

Like its sister-property Nikoi, Cempedak, which opened in 2017, was designed to be as self-sustaining as possible. Constructed with recycled and sustainable natural materials (such as bamboo), the resort's two-storey villas are open-sided to catch the sea breeze (negating the need for air-con) with extraordinary views over a marine conservation area-in waiting.

Two-thirds of the island remains virgin rainforest, which you can tour with flora and fauna experts – you may even be lucky enough to spot a critically endangered pangolin.

Cempedak has also established The Island Foundation that aims to engage the local community. Besides providing employment, Cempedak supports and cultivates local businesses (the resort's bamboo straws are made by a staff member's family) and educates staff, guests and future generations about the importance of protecting the environment.

$ *2-night stay for two from SGD$950*

🍴 *Indonesian fusion*

☞ *Riau Province; www.cempedak. com. The ferry, car and boat journey from Singapore to Cempedak island takes around 2½ hours*

7 WAYS TO REDUCE WASTE ON YOUR TRAVELS

Adopting a zero-waste mentality on the road can substantially mitigate your travel footprint, and your hosts will thank you later.

CHOOSE WASTE-CONSCIOUS TRANSPORT

Opt for airlines committed to reducing waste (the Qantas group plans to become the world's first airline to reuse, recycle and compost at least 75% of its waste by 2021). Bringing your own snacks and using your own headphones and eye-mask can also help to minimise in-flight waste.

PACK A ZERO-WASTE KIT

By travelling with a set of reusable alternatives to common single-use items such as coffee cups and plastic water bottles, bags, straws, and cutlery, you'll never get caught out having to use a disposable option. For destinations lacking safe drinking water, bring water purification tablets or a water filtration device, for example a LifeStraw (www.lifestraw.com).

OVERHAUL YOUR TRAVEL GEAR

Investing in good-quality travel gear made from natural fibres will help to limit the volume of harmful microfibres that end up in the delicate environments you visit when you do your laundry. And don't overlook your travel gadgets: head torches, for example, are now available in battery-free models, and a growing number of beauty brands sell plastic-free travel toiletries.

SHOP WISELY

Investing in souvenirs crafted from sustainable materials by local artisans not only helps to safeguard the environment and empower the preservation of cultural traditions, but meaningful souvenirs are also less likely to end up in the bin or at a charity shop back home.

BE ASSERTIVE

Get in the habit of requesting that food, drinks and other travel purchases are not served with disposable items such as plastic cutlery and bags before it's too late to hand them back. If queried why, embrace the opportunity to constructively raise awareness of the issue.

LEAN ON YOUR SMARTPHONE

There are dozens of apps and websites designed to help you limit your waste output, and maybe also save you money. In Australia, for example, www.responsiblecafes.org features an interactive map of coffee shops across the country that offer a discount for bringing your own cup. Also, instead of collecting brochures and flyers on the road (which inevitably get thrown out), use your phone's camera to take a snap instead.

GIVE BACK

Pay it forward to the places you visit by picking up litter during outdoor activities, and participating in community-led initiatives such as beach clean-ups.

INDONESIA
MISOOL ECO RESORT

● *Sleep in an overwater cottage in one of the world's best protected marine areas* ● *Indulge in traditional Indonesian wellness therapies* ● *Feast on sustainably caught seafood*

The 1500-odd islands that encompass the Raja Ampat archipelago are located at the centre of the Coral Triangle, a hotspot of marine biodiversity at the crossroads of the Pacific and Indian Oceans. This wild frontier off the west coast of New Guinea is often dubbed 'the Amazon of the sea' as it's home to 75% of the world's known coral species and nearly 1500 species of fish. Nowhere is it better protected than the Misool Private Marine Reserve, a 1220 sq km no-take zone set up by Misool Eco Resort and its charity arm, the Misool Foundation.

Dive trips don't get much better than this, and your money goes towards safeguarding one of the most beautiful reefs on Earth.

Misool's owners are firm believers that you can't protect nature without first empowering local communities to reclaim their traditional tenureship of reefs. That's why in addition to creating a shark and manta ray sanctuary, it also runs a community recycling project, has built a kindergarten, and also created programs to provide small loans for ex-manta and shark fin hunters to set up sustainable businesses.

Rooms at the eco-resort are either stilted overwater cottages or beachfront villas built entirely from reclaimed tropical hardwoods. In the wellness centre, you'll find only food-grade ingredients, so scrubs are hand-blended from native *kemiri* nuts or Papuan coffee beans, and body wraps are made from home-grown aloe plants or freshly harvested banana leaves. There are also cooking classes where you can work with the resort's chefs to make Balinese *sambal matah* (a lemongrass and chili dipping sauce), Sumatran rendang (a slow-cooked coconut curry) and pandan-scented crêpes.

$ *7-night stay per person incl meals and many activities from US$2400*

....

❙◉❙ *Organic and sustainably sourced Indonesian cuisine*

....

☛ *Raja Ampat; www. misool.info*

ITALY
LEFAY RESORT & SPA LAGO DI GARDA

● *Live la bella vita in a lavish lakeside resort with serious environmental credentials*
● *Dine on food made with ingredients grown right on the lakeshore*

Sustainability can be a driftwood bungalow on an empty beach or, in the case of Lefay Resort & Spa Lago di Garda, a stylish lakeside playground for socialites with a conscience. Set in 11 hectares of parkland, cascading down the hillside towards Lake Garda, the northern Italian resort is a modernist art deco homage, but behind the glamour is some serious eco-tech. With its swish interiors and fine-dining menus, Lefay is the embodiment of *la bella vita*, but

humming away quietly behind the scenes, a hidden power plant digests woodchips to heat the infinity pool, switching over to methane-fed micro-turbines for the cold north Italian winter. In summer, an absorption cooling system keeps guests as chilled as a freshly mixed Bellini.

Elegant rooms are set into the hillside beneath living green roofs, with silent radiant heating and cooling. Meals at the lemon-scented restaurant are crafted with local produce, including olive-oil pressed on the lakeshore, and the spa treatments make full use of local herbs and essences. And you can sleep easy too: bed linen is made from untreated natural fibres, and rooms are painted with environmentally friendly water-based paints.

Electricity, as you might expect, comes from renewable sources, but scanning systems monitor light levels across the complex to minimise the use of electric light. Sealing the deal, anything the resort can't minimise or avoid is offset by carbon credits; it's the best eco-efficient living money can buy.

ON YOUR DOORSTEP
Visible from almost every corner of the gorgeously landscaped grounds, the shimmering waters of Lake Garda call out like a beacon. To keep your carbon footprint low, skip the motorboat rides for wild swimming from the beaches at Sirmione, or windsurfing at Riva Del Garda.

$ *Doubles from €520*

🍽 *Modern Mediterranean cuisine*

☛ *Via Angelo Feltrinelli 136, Gargnano; https://lagodigarda.lefayresorts.com. Lefay Resort & Spa is accessible by taxi from the train station at Desenzano di Garda*

● **Eco-luxury** ● **Sustainable Dining** ● **Wellness**

JAMAICA
CAMP CABARITA WELLBEING ECO-RESORT

● *Shop at a local farmers market with resort chefs* ● *Indulge in a free coffee scrub or herbal soak* ● *Connect with nature on a hike to a tropical swimming hole*

Think of Camp Cabarita as an eco-luxe jungle camp for adults keen to connect with nature beyond Jamaica's beach resorts. Built with end-of-life trees on the property, it sits on the bank of the Cabarita River, with a riverside beach, swimming holes, and waterfalls all within walking distance. There are plenty of hammocks for everyone, and the open-air *shala* (studio) surrounded by old-growth jungle is the perfect spot for morning meditation classes.

Camp Cabarita is designed to be a place where guests can feel good about the ramifications of their presence. Here, you can pick your own fruits and veggies from the edible gardens, and food waste is composted. The resort also practises *hugukulture* (using decaying organic material for new-growth planting) and forest management, both of which you can learn about during your stay at this jungle paradise.

ON YOUR DOORSTEP
Camp Cabarita is a hub for outdoor adventure, from exploring caves to jumping off waterfalls. For travellers who prefer to keep it mellow, the farmers market in the nearby town of Savanna La Mar is worth a visit.

$ *Doubles incl meals per person US$135*

🍽 *Jamaican cuisine*

☞ *B9, Glenbrook; www.campcabarita. com. Cabarito is an hour's drive from Montego Bay; pick-ups can be arranged*

MADAGASCAR

EDEN LODGE

● *Taste locally made baobab juice or sherbet* ● *Spot wildlife galore beyond your glamping tent* ● *Start the day with an ocean kayak session and end it with a massage*

Imagine spotting migrating whales from your sunlounger, or perhaps a nocturnal lemur on your way to dinner. Accessible only by boat from the nearby island of Nosy Be, Eden Lodge's location on a remote beach in northwestern Madagascar makes it ideal for spotting the Indian Ocean nation's weird and wonderful endemic critters, from its 99 species of lemur to myriad parrots, and chameleons in every shape and colour. Offshore, colourful reefs teeming with marine life beckon snorkellers and divers.

Furnished with four-poster beds built from fallen trees and furnished with Malagasy crafts, rooms at the eco-luxe lodge – which claims to be the world's first solar-powered hotel – take the form of high-end safari tents nestled under traditional thatched-roof structures. The materials were sailed to the resort on traditional dhows to minimise carbon emissions, and a Ravenala tree (also known as the traveller's palm) is planted for each guest to further offset the impact. By using only solar power, buying local, and recycling wastewater rather than releasing it into the sea, Eden Lodge became the first hotel in Madagascar certified by international sustainability organisation Green Globe.

Between jungle hikes, scuba dives, natural massage treatments, and touring the region by boat, you can tuck into creative meals at the on-site restaurant created with all-local produce, including fish straight from the sea, and veggies from the organic garden.

ON YOUR DOORSTEP
Beach activities are complementary, and excursions to local fishing villages or island waterfalls are affordable and easily arranged. Be sure to spend an hour or so walking around the island's baobab tree grove; one massive tree is more than 700 years old.

$ *Doubles all-incl per person from €180*

🍽️ *French and traditional Malagasy cuisine*

☛ *Baobab Beach, Anjanojano; www. edenlodge.net*

MALAYSIA
FRANGIPANI LANGKAWI

● *Relax on the beach while 300 green measures tick along quietly in the background*
● *Enjoy organic breakfasts where even the fruit rinds are recycled*

Sustainability doesn't have to be in your face to be effective. Outwardly, Frangipani Langkawi ticks all the boxes for a typical Malay beach resort – tidy, tile-roofed villas scattered under the palms in a beach-side garden with multiple saltwater pools – but it's what goes on beyond the beach that's interesting.

The water that flows into each villa is purified using all-natural filtration by aquatic plants, dried casuarina leaves on the roof reduce the ambient temperature, and creepers climb the outside walls, reducing heat absorption. Even the rinds and peels from the morning organic fruit plates are rendered to make biodegradable detergents and natural pesticides. Environmental practices are so integral to the running of Frangipani Langkawi that guests hardly notice the 300 green policies the resort follows to keep each stay green, clean and serene.

ON YOUR DOORSTEP
The best strips of beach are crammed with resorts, but virgin rainforest cloaks the interior of Pulau Langkawi. Explore in futuristic fashion from the space-age skywalk atop Gunung Machincang (660m), or travel by boat into the mangroves of Kilim Karst Geoforest Park.

$ *Doubles from MYR472*

🍽 *Malaysian cuisine with local ingredients*

☛ *Pantai Tengah, Pulau Langkawi;* **www.frangipani langkawi.com. The island is accessible by boat from Kuala Perlis and Kuala Kedah**

MALAYSIA
GAYANA MARINE RESORT

● *Feast on sustainably harvested seafood at the pioneering on-site restaurant* ● *Lap up the marine park views from your overwater villa* ● *Get back to nature on a jungle hike*

There might be newer, glitzier resorts in Malaysia, but only Sabah's Gayana Marine Resort has its own research centre helping to save an endangered marine species.

Hugging the northeast coast of Pulau Gaya, just off Kota Kinabalu, the resort features 45 overwater villas constructed in harmony with the environment. At one end of the boardwalk linking the villas you'll find the Alu-Alu Chinese restaurant, among the nation's first to champion sustainable aquaculture. At the other end lies the Marine Ecology Research Centre (MERC) a research and rehabilitation facility specialising in the propagation of giant clams – which are endangered in Malaysia – and the restoration of coral reefs, with guests invited to assist in activities such as attaching coral fragments to an artificial reef. The resort has also banned plastic bottles, and operates a daily clean-up of ocean debris, adding additional feel-good factors to your stay.

ON YOUR DOORSTEP
Beyond snorkelling and diving, you can embark on a four-hour hike through the jungle (or take a short boat ride) to more luxe sister-resort Bunga Raya, where guests can access the resort's spa, restaurants, canopy walk and zipline.

$ *Villas from MYR1018*

🍽 *Chinese, Malay and international*

☛ *Gaya Island, Tunku Abdul Rahman NP, Sabah;* **www.echoresorts. com. Rates include scheduled 20-minute boat transfers from Kota Kinabalu**

MALDIVES

SONEVA FUSHI

● Enjoy a gourmet plant-based dinner in the resort's organic garden ● Recalibrate at the Maldives' most sustainable barefoot luxury hideaway ● Indulge in treatments at Six Senses spa

Since its first resort opened in 1972, the Maldives has had a fraught relationship with tourism. On one hand, it's the single greatest contributor to the economy. On the other, various studies have shown that the development and management of some resorts have contributed to the destruction of coral reefs that visitors come to see.

When he decided to open the Maldives' first luxury resort in 1995, Indian-British hotelier Sonu Shivdasani was adamant that sustainability would be at the heart of its ethos, from sourcing sustainable construction materials and maintaining the natural beauty of the resort's location (no trees were cut down) to working closely with local communities. Shivdasani was a true pioneer in the war against single-use plastics: toiletries were supplied in reusable earthenware jars from day one, and plastic straws were banned in 1998, followed by plastic bottles in 2008.

Today, Soneva is carbon-neutral, desalinates its own water, and recycles 90% of its waste on site. A permaculture-based organic garden produces ingredients for its restaurants, with other supplies sourced as sustainably as possible. And even after more than 20 years in operation, the 61-villa resort – situated in the Maldives' only Unesco Biosphere Reserve – remains one of the nation's top castaway escapes, with recent additions including its vegetarian restaurant Shades of Green and the world's first fully sustainable surfing programme.

ON YOUR DOORSTEP

Among its many activities, Soneva offers water-based experiences ranging from scuba diving and freediving to surfing and snorkelling with manta rays. You can also opt to enjoy a picnic on a private sandbar, take a sunset dolphin cruise, or simply stand-up paddleboard around the lagoon.

$ *Villa for two from US$1807*

 Gourmet multi-cuisine fare with homegrown produce

☞ **Kunfunadhoo Island, Baa Atoll; www.soneva.com**

MAURITIUS
OTENTIC ECO TENT EXPERIENCE

● *Experience Mauritius' only luxury glamping outfit* ● *Make your own cocktails with homemade rums* ● *Taste the freshness of homegrown vegetables*

Better known for its big luxury resorts, the island nation of Mauritius has a growing number of smaller, more sustainable accommodation options offering a more authentic island experience. Arguably the most characterful is Otentic, which runs two solar-powered glamping lodges on the island's east coast.

Spilling down a hillside next to a river that meets the sea, Otentic River is the more luxurious of the two. With huge private decks and sunken en-suite bathrooms, its 12 glamping tents, built entirely of wood and recycled materials, are set behind a wonderful communal outdoor area with a swimming pool, a lounge area, an honesty bar and a semi-al-fresco restaurant, which is also open to the public (bookings essential). By day, you can hang out by the pool, spot crimson red fody birds dart about the organic garden, or sign up for a free excursion to nearby island Ile aux Cerfs. You can also borrow a stand-up paddleboard or a kayak (included) to check out a small waterfall upriver, or perhaps set off for a hike in the mountains behind the lodge. Each evening, guests mingle around the outdoor firepit over drinks and canapes before tucking into a hearty dinner (MUR600) cooked by locals from nearby villages. Accompanied by salads and vegetables from the garden, the delicious Mauritian-style meals (think: creole-style calamari, sausage rougaille, and beef karri) are among the best you'll taste on the island.

ON YOUR DOORSTEP
From Mahebourg, a 45-minute drive south, take a tour of nearby Ile Aux Aigrettes with the Mauritian Wildlife Foundation (mauritian-wildlfe. org), which is working to save several endemic wildlife and plant species, including the critically endangered Mauritius olive white-eye.

$ *Per tent per night from MUR5000*

....

🍽 *Healthy, gourmet Mauritian fare*

....

☞ **Coastal Rd, Deux Freres, Grand River South East; www.otentic.mu**

MEXICO

HABITAS TULUM

● *Stay in a palapa-roof suite with ocean views and an outdoor rain shower* ● *Enjoy luxe spa treatments with detoxifying clay* ● *Savour seasonal and organic food sourced from local farms and fishers*

A beacon of environmental sustainability amid the ever-increasing development of Tulum, Habitas was designed to create the smallest footprint possible on its idyllic Yucatán Peninsula setting, with 3000 trees and shrubs planted on the pristine acre of beach it sits on for good measure.

Built in collaboration with local carpenters and artisans, Habitas' communal spaces were designed to encourage deeper human connection. The three-storey lobby is the heart of this convivial coastal retreat, a hub for both locals and travellers to convene at long tables made of reclaimed wood and seating areas with colorful pillows and low-bearing tables. Guests can also mingle with fellow travellers during daily rooftop yoga classes and at live music performances in the jungle courtyard cinema, where such films as *The Dark Side of Tulum* (2019) are screened to encourage necessary discussions about the ecological preservation of the Riviera Maya. When you need some private time, holistic spa treatments inspired by spiritual customs of the indigenous Maya culture are available at the on-site wellness centre.

Set amid jungle greenery and linked by stone pathways, the 32 bohemian-luxe guest rooms were built (on raised platforms) with indigenous materials such as palapa (for the thatched roofs). Private outdoor rain

$ *Doubles from US$300*

|O| *Spanish cuisine flavoured with North African spices*

☛ **Carretera Tulum-Bocapaila Km4, Quintana Roo; www. habitastulum.com. Shared shuttles ply the route from Cancùn to Habitas Tulum**

showers, plush robes and a custom-made line of bath products in reusable dispensers created with all-natural ingredients (coconut, avocado and honey) add to the luxe factor.

ON YOUR DOORSTEP
Complimentary bicycles provide a low-impact option for visiting local attractions, including the Maya ruins of Tulum (4km northeast). There's also Sian Ka'an Biosphere Reserve with its bevy of caves and cenotes you can swim, snorkel and dive in (7km south).

NEW ZEALAND
CAMP GLENORCHY

● *Recover from a long hike in a rustic-chic eco-cabin with plush eco-friendly furnishings*
● *Stock up on local, seasonal produce at the on-site grocery store*

Nestled in the foothills of the Southern Alps on New Zealand's South Island, at the head of Lake Wakatipu, lies the tiny village of Glenorchy. Best known as the gateway to the Routeburn Track, the picturesque town is also home to New Zealand's most sustainable visitor accommodation.

Designed, built and operated in line with the philosophy and principles of the International Living Future Institute's Living Building Challenge, recognised as the world's most stringent environmental building design certification, the 'camp', which opened in 2018, is a shining example of how comfort doesn't need to be sacrificed for sustainability. Beautifully furnished with original artworks, fine linens and luxe eco-friendly amenities, the cabins have an upscale country vibe. There's also cosy bunkrooms (NZ$75 per bed) and RV sites (NZ$75 per site), with camping available at next-door Mrs Wolly's, which is part of the same development.

While there's no restaurant, the on-site General Store is well-stocked with healthy local provisions to cook your food in the shared kitchen. Enjoy your meal in the mountain-view dining room, or perhaps by the campfire at the centre of the zero-net property, which uses as much energy it creates via its 'solar garden'. The best part? Camp Glenorchy's profits go to the local Glenorchy Community Trust to support initiatives that enhance the liveability and vibrancy of the town.

ON YOUR DOORSTEP
The trailhead of the Routeburn Track, one of New Zealand's Great Walks, is a 30-minute drive northwest of Glenorchy. Offering spectacular alpine vistas, the 33km trail is typically hiked over three days.

$ *Doubles from NZ$275*

🍽 *Cook up local produce in the communal kitchen*

☛ *34 Oban St, Glenorchy; www.theheadwaters.co.nz. Glenorchy is 45 minutes' drive northwest of Queenstown. Buses also operate on this route*

NEW ZEALAND'S OUTDOOR SAFETY CODE

With an average of five tramping deaths – and 4000 injuries – every year in New Zealand, preparation is key to responsible hiking. Reduce risk by adhering to the five elements of NZ's Outdoor Safety Code: plan your route, tell someone where you're going and when you're due back, be aware of the weather, know your limits, and take sufficient supplies.

NEW ZEALAND

HAPUKU LODGE & TREE HOUSES

● *Unwind in designer tree houses with mountain views* ● *Enjoy some of the best locally sourced food in New Zealand, some of it from Hapuku's 200-hectare property*

Created by a family of food-loving architects just outside Kaikoura, a little coastal town with a big environmentally conscious heart, Hapuku Lodge & Tree Houses was destined to be a special place. The luxury lodge with its two nature-inspired suites came first, in 2003, but the five designer tree houses built four years later really put Hapuku in a class of its own. Peaceful eyries of warmth and wood, they're 10m above the ground to take in views over the tops of 100-year-old native kanuka trees of the nearby Seaward Kaikoura mountain range and the Pacific Ocean.

The whole place is a model of sustainability – important in Kaikoura, a 'zero-waste community' that banned plastic bags way back in 2007 and is regularly EarthCheck-certified. Included in the room rates, gourmet dinners showcase the region's fresh local produce and seafood, including Kaikoura's famous crayfish, and venison – for in addition to having its own organic vegetable garden and olive trees, Hapuku happens to be a working deer farm.

Low-impact activities include beach and botanical walks, swimming in the solar-heated pool, biking mountain trails and scenic drives, while Mangamaunu surf break and Kaikoura's marine wonders are just down the road. Best of all, Hapuku plants native trees to offset guests' return flights to New Zealand, from anywhere in the world.

ON YOUR DOORSTEP

Love the sea? You'll love Kaikoura. A Māori-run whale-watching business (whalewatch.co.nz) put it on the tourist map in 1987 and it's still one of the best places in the world to see whales of all kinds and to swim with fur seals and huge pods of dusky dolphins.

$ *Doubles half-board from NZD$943*

🍴 *Locally sourced organic fine dining*

☛ **State Hwy 1 at Station Rd, RD1, Kaikoura; www. hapukulodge.com. Hapuku Lodge & Treehouses is on the east coast of New Zealand's South Island, 12km north of Kaikoura and a 2½-hour scenic drive or train ride north of Christchurch**

NICARAGUA

Isleta El Espino

● *Enjoy views of the Mombacho Volcano from a lush, private-island base* ● *Learn how to cook local specialities with homegrown produce* ● *Relax with private yoga classes overlooking Lake Nicaragua*

Serenity abounds at Isleta El Espino, a private tropical island in the northwest of Lake Nicaragua, the largest lake in Central America. Just a short boat ride from the charming colonial city of Granada, this five-room bohemian getaway is almost entirely self-sustainable, with the island's solar panels powering everything from lights and fans to systems that pump

and filter the swimming pool water. The owners even developed a filtration system to filter drinking water from Lake Nicaragua.

Guests can choose from two thatched-roof tree houses nestled in a mango grove, two secluded casitas (cabins) with outdoor decks, and an intimate bungalow built for two, each replete with polished concrete and wood floors, locally made hand-coloured cement tiles, and hand-loomed blankets and towels. Wood and stone walking paths lined with woven reed-and-clay lamps connect each room to the lodge's central area, where you'll find a swimming pool, a yoga platform, massage facilities, and an outdoor bar and palm-shaded restaurant. Visitors keen to connect with local culture can select from an array of experiences: learn how to make traditional Nicaraguan cuisine alongside the on-site chef with ingredients from the property's own organic herb and vegetable garden, or partake in a ceramic workshop with artists from the nearby town of San Juan de Oriente.

ON YOUR DOORSTEP
Book a four-hour hike to the top of the nearby Mombacho Volcano Nature Reserve (2344m) with the property's concierge to explore the crater, set within a protected cloud forest where sloths, monkeys, and the endemic Mombacho salamander roam.

$ *Doubles from US$125*

🍽 *Nicaraguan dishes enhanced by island-grown ingredients*

☞ **Las Isletas de Granada; www.isletaelespino.com. Rates include boat transfers (10 minutes each way) from Marina Cocibolca, 6km south of central Granada**

NORWAY
SVART

● *Bed down in the world's first energy-positive hotel – in the Arctic* ● *Harvest local delicacies and participate in the preparation of your own meals* ● *Practise yoga in the midnight sun*

High up in the Arctic Circle, nestled at the base of Norway's Svartisen glacier, the world's first energy-positive hotel is taking shape. Set to open in 2021, Svart is designed to use 85% less energy than normal hotels. It's named in tribute to the deep blue ice of Norway's second-largest glacier (svart means 'black' in Norwegian), and will feature solar panels on the roof and heating provided by geothermal wells.

Inspired by the *fiskehjell* – a wooden structure used by fishers in Norway to dry fish – the luxury hotel's circular design and large windows will allow guests to enjoy 360-degree views of the fjords, glaciers and mountains, while also optimising sunlight to the rooms and restaurants throughout the seasons.

And while it would be tempting to spend your stay soaking up the views, guests are encouraged to head outdoors, with activities set to include glacier walking, ice climbing, fishing, kayaking, and even scuba diving. Wintertime will offer prime Northern Lights viewing, while in summer you'll be able to practise yoga under the midnight sun.

¶◉ı *Gourmet Nordic cuisine*

☛ *Nordland; www.*
svart.no. The hotel
can only be accessed
by boat, with an
energy-neutral boat
shuttle expected to
operate from the city
of Bodø

A RENEWABLE FUTURE

The Nordic region is the poster child for the environmental and economic benefits of embracing renewable energy. Since 2000, the combined economies of Åland, Denmark, Faroe Islands, Finland, Greenland, Iceland, Norway and Sweden have grown by 28%, while carbon emissions have fallen by 18%. All regions have policies to be practically fossil fuel free by 2050.

OMAN

Six Senses Zighy Bay

● *Feast on haute cuisine fresh from the on-site permaculture garden* ● *Kick back in a sustainably constructed luxury villa* ● *Sign up for a facial with products blended with indigenous ingredients*

Six Senses is known for building ultra-sustainable luxury resorts in some of the world's most beautiful and remote locations, and Zighy Bay does not let the boutique hotel brand down. Wedged between a turquoise bay and the dramatic Western Hajar mountains, this village-style resort is the stuff of desert dreams. Think: spacious villas built with natural stone and warm woods, each opening out onto a private pool, and your own Guest Experience Maker who can arrange anything from snorkelling trips to guided hikes to a hammam-style scrub down at the tranquil Six Senses Spa.

The hotel's sustainability initiatives makes the experience even sweeter. In line with its zero-waste philosophy, single-use plastics are a thing of the distant past, and hotel waste is upcycled in a variety of ways, with landscaping waste fed to milk-producing goats, and food waste is used to compost the organic permaculture-style garden. Like all Six Senses properties, the resort has its own reverse osmosis plant for purifying water (guests are provided with reusable bottles) and alternatives to palm oil and soy products – which are responsible for deforestation around the world – are used in the kitchens of its three restaurants. Guests are invited to learn more at the hotel's Earth Lab, where the resort showcases its efforts to reduce its consumption and reliance on external resources, and support communities and ecosystems.

ON YOUR DOORSTEP

The Musandam Peninsula has some of the best scuba diving in the Middle East, and divers can help specially trained dive hosts to remove ghost nets left by fishers, and rescue sea creatures that have been caught in them.

$ *Doubles from US$772*

🍽 *Regional and international fine dining*

☛ **Musandam Peninsula; www. sixsenses.com**

PHILIPPINES

Bravo Resort

● *Sip plastic-free cocktails by the sea* ● *See the island's green movement in action at this stylish central resort* ● *Relax on your private leafy terrace*

With its pumping surf, idyllic beaches and lagoons, and an interior blanketed in lush coconut palms and rice paddies so green they almost glow, it's a miracle the remote Philippine island of Siargao is still (at least for now) one of the most wonderfully low-key tourism destinations in the country. Central to its appeal is its eco-conscious vibe. United by the Siargao Environmental Awareness (SEA) Movement, an impressive number of tourism businesses (in the main tourist hub of General Luna and beyond) have banned single-use plastics and committed to minimising their footprint in a variety of other ways.

In the heart of General Luna, just steps from the beach, Bravo Resort is a prime example. Conscious of the island's ongoing waste management issues, this stylish small resort crushes glass bottles into sand (which is then used for construction), meticulously separates garbage for recycling, and composts food waste. Guests also receive a reusable water bottle to use during their stay (with water refill stations in the reception area and restaurant) and they'll even give you a 400 peso refund for every night you surrender your air-con controller and opt to use the fan instead. The rooms (including a 'surf bunk' dorm) are among the nicest on the island. And set back from the turquoise sea in a breezy traditional-style pavilion, Bravo's excellent bar also makes a mean pina colada – sans plastic straw, of course.

ON YOUR DOORSTEP
Bravo Resort is the launch point for a variety of excellent, eco-friendly tours run by My Siargao Guide (facebook.com/mysiargaoguide), including an island-hopping tour with healthy and delicious plastic-free catering.

$ *Doubles from PHP3900*

🍽 *Spanish and international*

☛ *Tourism Rd, General Luna, Siargao del Norte; www.bravosiargao. com*

PHILIPPINES
TAO

● *Sail between tropical islands, stopping off for massages provided by a women's collective* ● *Fill up on delicious meals with produce from Tao's organic farm*

What began as an adventure of exploration in northern Palawan on an old fishing boat has evolved into one of the world's most incredible island-hopping experiences. Meaning 'people' in Filipino, Tao specialises in three- and five-day boat expeditions in one of the most stunning and remote corners of the Philippines. As the name suggests, people are at the heart of Tao, from the fun-loving local 'Lost Boys' who crew expedition boats, to the communities en route that Tao supports through various projects, such as a women's association which trains massage therapists and runs sewing workshops. With no set itinerary, expedition boats (each with its own canine first mate) travel between the tourism hubs of Coron and El Nido, with days spent cruising between pristine snorkelling spots and deserted beaches untouched by mass tourism. Each afternoon, 'explorers' disembark at one of 13 Tao camps scattered throughout the archipelago to sleep in simple bamboo huts and eat like castaway kings and queens. Most expeditions spend one night at the Tao Farm, which doubles as a training centre for staff and houses an organic farm,

reducing Tao's reliance on imported produce. To further minimise the company's environmental impact, Tao expeditions are single-use plastic-free and food is never wasted, with leftovers creatively morphed into delicious snacks. With few creature comforts, this adventure isn't for everyone, though former explorers will tell you they wished it would never end.

ON YOUR DOORSTEP
Coron is famed for its WWII wreck-diving opportunities, while El Nido has some of the Philippines' best beaches and kayaking. Don't forget your reusable water bottle, as plastic bottles are now banned on El Nido tours.

$ *5-day boat expedition incl meals from US$545*

🍽 *Healthy Filipino fusion*

☛ **Offices in Coron and El Nido, Palawan; www. taophilippines.com. Boat expeditions run at least once weekly (October to August) between Coron town and El Nido in Palawan province, and vice versa**

PUERTO RICO

FINCA VICTORIA

● *Stay in an ocean-view tree house* ● *Mix your own essential oils and healing balms*
● *Enjoy daily vegetarian breakfast feasts in an open-air wooden cabana*

Puerto Rican native and hotelier Sylvia DeMarco opened Finca Victoria on Vieques, a secluded island off Puerto Rico's eastern coast, as a low-impact sanctuary for travellers in need of a soulful respite. Nestled in the mountains in the island's central west with views of both the ocean and countryside, this farmhouse-style B&B offers guests a chance to slow down and savour the natural wonders of this Caribbean isle, whether that be kayaking across a bioluminescent bay, lazing on white-sand beaches where wild horses roam, or listening to an evening symphony of native coqui frogs beneath a sky so dark the Milky Way pops.

Set on one of the highest points in Vieques and almost exclusively powered by solar panels, Finca Victoria offers spacious suites and tiny homes – plus Bauhaus-inspired, two-storey tree houses with large balconies, outdoor showers, and high wood-beam ceilings for cross-ventilation. All are decorated with vintage furniture and works by Puerto Rican artists, and have translucent roofs to welcome the island's natural surrounds within.

At the heart of the property is the retreat's central wooden loft and cabana – an open-air living room decorated in retro furnishings, where guests can enjoy complimentary vegetarian or vegan breakfasts made with ingredients sourced from the property's own

organic Ayurvedic garden, which also provides herbs for an essential-oil station offering water infusions, teas and healing balms used in the myriad spa treatments, ranging from reflexology massages to cranial-sacral bodywork treatments. It overlooks a freshwater pool and sundeck framed by hammocks where guests can gather for morning yoga classes.

$ *Doubles from US$119*

....

🍽 *Ayurvedic and Caribbean vegetarian and vegan cuisine*

....

☛ *Route 995, Km2.2, Vieques; www. lafinca.com. The island of Vieques can be reached by a 45-minute passenger ferry from the mainland*

PUERTO RICO
HIX ISLAND HOUSE

● *Bed down in a uniquely designed, spacious guesthouse that lets the outside in*
● *Zen-out at a daily yoga class* ● *Start the day with organic eggs your way*

At this hilltop eco-retreat in Vieques – a diminutive Caribbean island 13km east of Puerto Rico's mainland – Canadian architect John Hix has created a one-of-a-kind hotel that takes its design cue from the landscape, the sun, the rain and the trade winds. Surrounded by lush vegetation, 18 loft-style rooms are spread over four stark yet beautiful concrete casas, Rectangular, Triangular and Redonda (each named after their geometric forms) and Casa Solaris, the first hotel accommodation in the Caribbean that's entirely off-the-grid – all work in harmony with the giant granite boulders that dot the hillside.

The hurricane-proof structures blend sustainability with contemporary tropical modern design. There's no need for air-con – with no glass, the minimalist lofts are open to the elements. The sun powers the electricity and heats the water. You can shower under the sun or stars with environmentally friendly toiletries, and the water is recycled to nourish the guavas and papayas growing in the garden. And there are no TVs, just views stretching over tropical greenery to the blues of the Caribbean.

There's no restaurant or bar either but you get a fully equipped kitchen – all the appliances are energy efficient – and all the ingredients (including organic eggs, just-baked bread and tropical fruit) to rustle up a hearty breakfast, washed down with Puerto Rican coffee.

The island is home to astoundingly beautiful beaches and great snorkelling spots, but for lazy days there's a stunning 50ft pool to lounge by, and daily yoga classes in the open-sided yoga pavilion.

ON YOUR DOORSTEP
Take a kayak tour of one of Vieques' most unique nature reserves. Bahía Mosquito Bioluminescent Bay has one of the highest concentrations of phosphorescent dinoflagellates in the world and any movement in the water whips up fluorescent-blue sparkles below the surface.

$ *Doubles from US$115*

|●| *Cook your own organic breakfast*

☛ Km 1.5, Route 995, Vieques; www. hixislandhouse.com. The island of Vieques can be reached by a 45-minute passenger ferry from the mainland

SOUTH AFRICA
GROOTBOS PRIVATE NATURE RESERVE

● *Enjoy a massage in the milkwood forest* ● *Sample local wine on a picnic amid the fynbos*
● *Stay in a luxurious suite immersed in nature* ● *Take a luxury African safari of another kind*

Grootbos is not a typical South African reserve with apex predators mooching about the bush. Instead, this 25 sq km nature reserve makes the most of its position near Africa's southernmost point, Cape Agulhas, where the meeting of the Atlantic and Indian Oceans creates a nutrient-rich Serengeti of the sea. Join marine biologists on an eco-friendly boat to see the Marine Big Five (whales, sharks, dolphins, seals and penguins). The indigenous fynbos surrounding Grootbos' forest suites is equally biodiverse. This is the Cape Floral Kingdom, the smallest and richest of the world's six Unesco-protected floral kingdoms, with more biodiversity between Table Mountain and the Garden Route than the Amazon.

Established in 1994, the reserve is one of 10 Global Ecosphere Retreats in the Long Run network founded by German sustainable business guru Jochen Zeitz and his Zeitz Foundation. Long Run members follow Zeitz' philosophy of developing tourism sustainably through the '4Cs' – conservation, community, culture and commerce. What this means for guests is an exclusive eco-retreat with secluded contemporary suites offering sweeping views of mountain-fringed Walker Bay, underpinned by an ethos of protecting its remarkable environment and empowering surrounding communities. The owners established the Grootbos Foundation in 2003 to conserve the critically endangered fynbos and focus on the skills development of locals. Among its awards, Grootbos won the Best Ecologically Responsible category at the Safari Awards 2019, the industry gold standard for wildlife travel businesses worldwide.

ON YOUR DOORSTEP
Just down the road in Gansbaai is the African Penguin & Seabird Sanctuary (dict.org.za), which rehabilitates local marine avian species, and is free to visit. To the north, Stony Point Nature Reserve in Betty's Bay is home to one of the largest breeding colonies of African penguins.

$ *Doubles all-incl from ZAR11,480*

🍽 *Locally inspired organic gastronomy*

☛ **Gansbaai, Western Cape; www. grootbos.com**

SRI LANKA
HERITANCE TEA FACTORY

● *Unwind in front of tea plantation views in a heritage hotel focused on sustainability*
● *Enjoy treatments based on traditional therapies and organic herbs, essences and oils*

Heritance Tea Factory wears its history on its sleeve. Relics from its past as the century-old Hethersett Tea Factory spill out into rooms and shared spaces – a sifting machine here, a train carriage from the old plantation railway there. But this is heritage with ethics: the hotel has a commendable commitment to sustainability and environmental practices. Cooking ingredients are sourced from an organic garden, tea comes from the hotel's organic tea plants, rainwater is conserved, solar panels heat the showers, and energy is produced using carbon-efficient biomass gasification. Highly trained staff from local villages keep these initiatives ticking along subtly in the background, leaving guests free to indulge in Sri Lankan-inspired spa treatments and admire the scenery – a lush carpet of rolling hills covered in a lace-like tracery of tea bushes.

ON YOUR DOORSTEP
With a working tea estate right on your doorstop, plantation walks and tea tasting are popular ways to unwind. Guests can even learn how to harvest tea leaves from local pickers and take home a packet of self-plucked tea.

$ *Doubles from US$167*

◉ *International and Sri Lankan food*

☛ *Kandapola, Nuwara Eliya; www.heritancehotels.com/teafactory. Take a train from Colombo to Nuwara Eliya, then it's a 13km taxi ride to the hotel*

● Eco-luxury ● Sustainable Dining ● Wellness

SWITZERLAND
WHITEPOD

● *Combine futuristic modernity with pristine nature, staying in a geodesic dome* ● *Feast on homemade Swiss treats, including grand desserts* ● *Unwind with wellness treatments using local floral oils.*

With its of cluster of futuristic geodesic domes spilling down a lush hillside in the heart of the Swiss Alps, staying at the Whitepod feels a little like being the first terraformer to set up base on a distant planet. Though it would have to be a pretty special planet to match the alpine views afforded from these unique sleeping pods, left bare and gleaming white in winter, and covered to blend into the landscape in summer. A pioneer of the eco-pod movement, Whitepod replaces lavish hotel luxuries with simplicity: uncluttered spaces, panoramic natural views, serene silence and the warm glow of an environmentally friendly pellet-burning stove. Water and energy use are minimised, recycling is maximised, and food is sourced locally, often from within the same valley. Add family-focused farm visits, guided walks, foraging, and winter sports and it's the perfect alpine eco-package.

ON YOUR DOORSTEP
Mountain guides are on hand to lead you into the hills, where you can collect therapeutic alpine herbs. In winter, ski touring and snowshoe hiking is possible right from the terrace in front of each pod.

$ *2-night stay for 2 CH900*

◉ *Seasonal Swiss*

☛ *Les Cerniers, Les Giettes, Valais; www.whitepod.com. Trains run from Zürich and Geneva to Monthey, from where you can transfer to Whitepod by taxi in around 15 minutes*

THAILAND

GOLDEN BUDDHA BEACH RESORT

● *Go upmarket Robinson Crusoe, staying in elegant wood cabins on a tropical island with more monkeys than people* ● *Enjoy curries made with coconut milk from the palms swaying overhead*

On a proper beach escape, you don't have to share the sand. At Golden Buddha Beach Resort, there are 12 unspoiled kilometres of the stuff, and few other people to disturb the views of sand, surf and sea. Ko Phra Thong is home to just a handful of villages, inhabited by Moken fishers and their families, and upmarket castaways at Golden Buddha have the island mostly to themselves, staying in handsome Thai-style cottages dotted between the melaleuca trees. Behind this coastal strip stretches a serene and sunlit savannah, one of the last refuges for the lesser adjutant stork, and a playground for monkeys, slow lorises and pangolins. Golden Buddha's eco-credentials also stand up to scrutiny: showers are heated by solar panels, drinking water is purified on site, waste is composted or transported for proper disposal at facilities on the mainland, ingredients are local (including fruit from an organic orchard) and dishes are washed in homemade orange-peel detergent. Even the coconut milk in the Thai curries is produced from local trees. And the resort is firmly plugged into the local community – 90% of staff come from the island, transport and boat trips are run by village families, and the resort funds the island's only school – so you can feel good about getting away from it all.

ON YOUR DOORSTEP

If you tire of the sand, Ko Phra Thong is flanked to the north and east by densely forested islands and inlets, and there are kayaks and stand-up paddleboards for self-guided exploring. And the diving and snorkelling playground of the Surin Islands lies just 50km offshore.

$ *3-night stay for two people THB22,800*

....

।◉। *Homemade Thai cuisine*

....

☛ **131 Moo 2, Thanon Ko Phra Thong, Phang-Nga; www. goldenbuddharesort. com. Longtail boats can be chartered to the resort from Kuraburi pier, north of Phuket. It's best to make arrangements with the resort as boaters may not speak English**

UK
SWINTON BIVOUAC

● *Connect with nature at well-thought-out mindfulness retreats, and revel in the noise-free environment* ● *Cosy up in an atmospheric tree lodge decked out with fairy lights and log burners*

If woodland fairies exist, they are surely resident around Swinton Bivouac. A string of tree lodges guards the forest edge, where a valley sweeps down to a huddle of meadow yurts and a cafe converted from a barn. Paths crowded with conifers, wild mushrooms and the occasional marsh orchid lead to a druid's temple cocooned in the woods – an 18th-century folly built by the owners of the country estate (complete with a Grade II-listed castle) that hosts this glamping site.

Not only is it a magical place, but Swinton Bivouac is one of England's most sustainable

boltholes. The accommodation is completely off-grid, illuminated by candles and log fires at night. The tree houses have been built using sustainable materials from the Swinton estate and are insulated with wool sourced from nearby Cumbria. A carbon-neutral wood-chip boiler provides all of the site's heating and hot water, while a grey water system recycles throughout the site. Families love it here, and dogs are welcomed, too.

Swinton Bivouac is far from the madding crowds and human sounds are a rarity. This is partly why it makes such a perfect location for wellness retreats focusing on digital detoxing and reconnecting with nature. Launched in 2019, these two-day retreats (£375 all-incl) are led by Forest Bathing UK founder Faith Douglas, a brilliant guide in the art of how to 'just be'. Participants experience sound baths, silent forest walks and reiki drumming around the campfire. Guests staying at other times of year can instead join her for mindful walks in the estate gardens, next to Swinton Park's swanky spa.

ON YOUR DOORSTEP
Stargazing, hiking, biking and caving are just a few of the activities on offer in the nearby Yorkshire Dales National Park. At a pinch, it's walkable to the village of Masham, home to two famous family breweries – Theakston and Black Sheep – with tours and tastings.

$ *Doubles from £109*

🍽 *Cafe grub, and vegetarian and vegan during retreats*

☛ ***Swinton Park Estate, England; www.swintonestate. com/bivouac. Swinton Park Estate is on the edge of the Yorkshire Dales National Park, a 30-minute drive from the nearest train station at Thirsk. Porters from the estate can sometimes provide lifts***

VANUATU

Ratua Island Resort & Spa

● *Experience barefoot luxury in beachfront teak villas* ● *Enjoy gourmet meals showcasing organic 'zero kilometre' produce* ● *Bliss out in the antique overwater spa villa*

Imagine owning a tropical island. What would you do with it? If you're like philanthropic French couple Marc and Isabelle Hénon, who created Ratua Island Resort in 2010, you'd do this: bring in some 200-year-old Javanese teak villas, decorate them with sumptuous soft furnishings and objets d'art you'd collected on your travels, make the whole place environmentally and socially sustainable and throw open its wooden-latched doors to those seeking an eco-chic refuge from 21st century life.

Ratua is the epitome of barefoot luxury. There are no room keys, no meal times, no rules. It's a place for low-impact lazing – swimming a few steps from your beachfront villa, snorkelling with turtles, riding horses and mountain bikes – and for dining on the beach by candlelight on freshly caught lobster, sipping pina coladas from just-fallen coconuts and wriggling your toes in the warm sand.

There's a zero-plastic policy, wooden ceiling fans in each of the 14 villas instead of air-con, and plans to go carbon neutral. And almost everything you eat is from the sea or the island's organic garden, orchard or livestock (free-range beef cattle, pigs and chickens); even the wines come from the owners' vineyard in France.

Most importantly, and refreshingly, staying at Ratua helps local communities, particularly their children, because 100% of the resort's profits go directly to the Ratua Foundation, making this the ultimate feel-good sustainable stay.

ON YOUR DOORSTEP
Espiritu Santo's natural delights are a short boat ride away, including world-famous dive sites Million Dollar Point and the SS *President Coolidge*; Champagne Beach, where tiny volcanic gas bubbles make the water sparkle; and the Blue Hole, an ethereal freshwater swimming spot.

$ *2-night stay for two from VUV116,000*

....

🍽 *Fresh, organic, Pacific Rim cuisine*

....

☞ *Ratua Island; www.ratua.com. Ratua. Ratua Island is a 35-minute boat ride from Luganville on Espiritu Santo, Vanuatu's largest island*

VIETNAM
MANGO BAY RESORT

● *Support the conservation of a Vietnamese national park as you soak up the sun, sea and sand in eco-luxe digs* ● *Indulge in a spa treatment with products made from 100% natural ingredients*

The owners of Mango Bay believe in taking care of their own backyard. Half of Phu Quoc island is set aside as a national park, and the resort invests a share of its takings to support a broad sweep of environmental initiatives, from conservation projects and biodiversity surveys to replanting native Vietnamese plants and trees.

Guests still get the full beach resort experience – ocean sunsets, golden sand, fresh seafood from the bay – but a lot of thought has gone into minimising the resort's environmental impact. The huge, airy cabins are designed to maximise natural airflow, avoiding the need for air-con, and water is pumped and treated from shallow wells in the grounds. It's a great example of joined-up thinking – the resort uses only natural lighting during the day and even the minibar comes in a cool-box, not a power-thirsty refrigerator.

ON YOUR DOORSTEP
Phu Quoc National Park is on the resort's doorstep. Explore by raft, kayak or on foot and you may bump into great hornbills, silvered langurs, slow lorises and small-clawed otters, plus a legion of macaques and fruit bats.

$ *Doubles VDN3,662,000*

|❍| *Vietnamese/Thai*

☛ ***Ong Lang Beach, Phu Quoc, Kien Giang; www.mango bayphuquoc.com. Get there by fast ferry from Ha Tien and Rach Gia***

- Community Interaction
- Arts & Traditions
- Homestays

CULTURE

AUSTRALIA

WUKALINA WALK

● *Learn the stories of Tasmanian Aboriginals during a multi-day hike in their cultural homeland* ● *Learn how to identify bush tucker and weave a basket from kelp*

Known for its fiery lichen-tinged granite headlands, impossibly white sandy beaches and idyllic turquoise water, northeastern Tasmania's Bay of Fires is one of Australia's most incredible natural landscapes. With several popular hiking trails in the region, it's a fantastic place to get back to nature. But if you opt for the Wukalina Walk, you can also learn about the 10,000-odd years of Aboriginal history and culture connected to the region.

Launched in 2018, the Wukalina Walk is Tasmania's first *palawa* (Tasmanian Aboriginal) owned and operated guided walk. The first time *palawa* people have had the chance to tell their story, on their own land, and in their own

time, the three-day, four-night exploration of the Larapuna (Bay of Fires) and Wukalina (Mt William) areas is a genuine cultural experience guaranteed to deepen your understanding of *palawa* culture and community history. Immersing you in the natural and rugged beauty of the breathtaking coastal region, the 34km walk sees guests spend two nights lodging in comfortable bespoke domed huts and one night in the luxuriously renovated Lighthouse Keepers Cottage at Eddystone Point. Walking in the footsteps of your guide's ancestors (keep your eye out for wildlife), you will hear first-hand creation stories and participate in cultural practices that have been passed down for hundreds of generations, with evenings spent dining on traditional produce, chatting with Aboriginal Elders, spotting nocturnal wildlife, and sipping fine Tasmanian wine.

ON YOUR DOORSTEP

For additional insight into Tasmania's Aboriginal history, don't miss 'The First Tasmanians' exhibition at the Queen Victoria Art Gallery at Royal Park in Launceston, which features rarely seen original objects and examines climate change, astronomy and stories of creation, craft, and more.

$ *4-day walk (www. wukalinawalk.com.au) all-incl from AU$2495*

🍴 *Tasmanian recipes prepared with local produce and native ingredients*

☞ **The guided walk (available October through April) departs from and ends at the Tasmanian Aboriginal Elders Council of Tasmania Centre in Launceston**

BHUTAN

WANGCHUCK CENTENNIAL NATIONAL PARK HOMESTAY

● Experience life in a traditional rammed earth Bhutanese home ● Learn to live in harmony with the landscape from Himalayan yak herders ● Support the preservation of local traditions

The beauty of the Bhutanese model for tourism, once you get over the shock of the US$200-250 daily fee, is that you're fully in control of your own destiny. You can tell your guide to follow the well-trodden trail through Paro, Thimphu and Punakha, or veer off into frontier country, staying with villagers in the wildlands of Wangchuck Centennial National Park. Covering 4919 sq km of middle Himalayan biome, this rugged reserve takes in everything from high-altitude snowfields to dense forests, providing a home for remote farming communities and semi-nomadic herders, alongside sizable populations of tigers, snow leopards, bears and takin (Bhutanese antelope).

Preserving both wildlife populations and human livelihoods is the mission of the homestay programme founded by the World Wildlife Fund and Bhutan's royal family, allowing income from tourism to offset the losses to crops and livestock caused by park wildlife. Staying in gateway villages such as Nasiphel and Ngalakha, travellers directly contribute to conservation, supporting a way of life that is vanishing as younger villagers abandon the mountains for Bhutan's cities.

In a traditional rammed earth home, activity is focused on the wood-burning *bukhari* stove in the kitchen, where the owners churn salted butter tea and dry strips of *shakam* (beef jerky). You might be asked to help drive wild boar from the fields, or join an impromptu game of *khuru* (Bhutanese darts). It's an experience far removed from the hotel buffets and spa baths on a standard tour of Bhutan.

ON YOUR DOORSTEP

Wangchuck Centennial National Park encompasses a vast swathe of mountain terrain. With a local guide, you can seek out rare wildlife or trek to meditation caves, glacial lakes and ancient ruins in the hills.

$ Per day all-incl per person around US$250; find operators through the Tourism Council of Bhutan; www.tourism.gov.bt

🍴 Bhutanese cooking

☞ *Wangchuck Centennial National Park. The best gateway to Wangchuck is Bumthang. You'll have a vehicle as part of an organised trip (a condition of visiting Bhutan), but some villages are only accessible on foot.*

THE TOURISM MODEL OF THE FUTURE?

Bhutan adheres to a policy of 'high value, low impact' tourism, requiring all visitors to book a guide, and spend at least US$200 per day. But while this may seem expensive, when you consider that the day rate includes three-star accommodation, all meals, a licensed guide, camping equipment and land transport, it's actually a very competitive deal.

CANADA

Atikamekw Nation Cultural Immersion

● *Learn about Canadian First Nations culture by staying with a community on Atikamekw Nation land* ● *Learn to make traditional crafts* ● *Stay in teepees*

It's unknown for exactly how long the Atikamekw people have been in the forests north of Montreal – after all, they have no written history – but mentions of the tribe start appearing in French documents from the early 1600s. Amazingly, 400 years later, the Atikamekw still live in the same area as their ancestors and have preserved a remarkable number of skills and traditions. Located in Manawan, this current generation of First Nations people live by a code similar to their ancestors, prioritising resource management and living with the seasons.

The Atikamekw community in Matawan also opens its doors to visitors via a three-day site visit programme. Guests stay in teepees near Lake Kempt with members of the Atikamekw Nation, spending days learning Atikamekw traditions and skills, and evenings stargazing and listening to Native American legends around a campfire. Meals, too, are Atikamekw; moose meat paired with seasonal produce is common, though vegetarian options are available.

In the spring, you can opt for a two-night visit, including lessons on sugar collection methods and a stay at the Atikamekw-owned inn in Matawan. There's also a five-night option in August that offers the opportunity to attend the Atikamekw annual pow-wow celebration and participate in native crafts, arts, dance, and cooking.

All programmes are run and hosted by members of the Atikamekw Nation, with 100% of the cost supporting the community, many members of whom rely on tourism funds to support their otherwise traditional lifestyles.

ON YOUR DOORSTEP
While staying at the camp, active travellers can choose to hike with a local foraging expert to learn about medicinal plants or paddle in a wooden canoe past beaver dams.

$ *3-day programme per person from CAD$440*

🍽 *Traditional Atikamekw Nation cuisine*

☛ *Communauté Atikamekw De Manawan, Baie-Atibenne, Quebec; www. voyageamerindiens. com. The programme is held in Manawan, a community on Atikamekw Nation land*

CUBA

LAS TERRAZAS

● *Visit Cuba's first community tourism project* ● *Hop between resident artists' studios* ● *Stay in local homes – a Cuba travel rite of passage*

It's difficult to imagine that 50 years ago Las Terrazas was a barren land, following years of industrial abuse which stripped it of its resources. A campaign under Fidel Castro began in 1968 to re-wild the area and employ its impoverished inhabitants, who planted seven million trees in a matter of years. So successful was the reforestation that in 1984 Unesco gave biosphere status to 267 sq km of land around Las Terrazas, creating the Sierra del Rosario Biosphere Reserve. By the early 1990s the eco-community needed another purpose, so tourism was developed.

Today Las Terrazas is home to 1000 Cubans, but still feels like an unobtrusive blip in the naval of the reserve. Rivulets of whitewashed homes crowned with terracotta roofs barely dent the thickets of palms and bromelias. Undulating hills and a central lagoon add to its topographical charms.

The establishment of tourism accommodation in the form of *casas particulares* (homestays), rustic cabins and a pioneering Cuban eco-hotel called Moka has provided residents with an economic lifeline: almost two-thirds now work in tourism. A 1.6km zipline through the forest canopy is a key attraction, and there's also kayaking, birdwatching and hiking. Another of the community's USPs is its artists' studios surrounding the lake. A handful of Cuban painters and artisans have been drawn here by the inspirational setting, creating a vibrant network of open galleries and giving visitors the chance to interact with artists who have been energised by the landscape.

ON YOUR DOORSTEP

In the centre of the village, the Callejón de la Moka sells locally made artworks, essential oils and perfumes. Lestér Campa's waterfront studio exhibits art (for sale) that channels the environment of Las Terrazas. You can also visit the home of Terrazas-born musician Polo Montañez (1955–2002), now a museum.

$ *Cabins for two from €25*

|O| *Affordable local Cuban dishes*

← Las Terrazas, Artemisa; www. lasterrazas.cu. Las Terrazas is 60km west of Havana and it takes 75 minutes to get there by Viazul bus

ECUADOR

YUNGUILLA COMMUNITY TOURISM PROJECT

● *Visit one of Ecuador's longest running community tourism projects* ● *Hike the cloud forest with a local guide* ● *Eat with local families and stay in their homes*

A pioneer in community tourism in Ecuador, the village of Yunguilla sits in a cloud forest, 90 minutes north of the capital Quito. The region had previously been part of a large hacienda, farmed in a traditional feudal system. In the 1990s, a group of residents launched a cooperative venture to make the community more economically sustainable and to restore the region's natural environment, which had suffered significant deforestation. And while other residents dubbed this group '*los locos*' (the crazy ones), they succeeded in developing one of Ecuador's longest running community tourism projects.

Residents set up a cheese- and yogurt-making facility and a small operation to produce marmalade from *uvillas* (gooseberries), blackberries, and other local fruits. They planted trees to bring the native forest, as well as a large organic garden, where they grow cabbage, corn, potatoes, and many types of greens and herbs. And they began offering environmentally focused tours and opening their homes to visitors.

Today, you can come to Yunguilla for a day or more to learn about the community and to hike through the lush forest with a resident guide, on the lookout for native birds and flowers, including many varieties of colourful orchids. You can have lunch in the community restaurant, with sweeping views across the valley, and a number of families provide meals and accommodation in their sturdy wooden homes. As you get acquainted with your hosts, you might enjoy soup made with local greens, locally raised chicken, and potatoes from the organic garden, before settling in for the night, listening to the chirps and tweets from the revitalised cloud forest.

$ *1-night experience incl full board per person from US$90*

❍| *Simple Ecuadorian meals in homestays or at the community restaurant*

☛ Yunguilla; www. yunguilla.org.ec. From Ofelia station in north Quito, catch a public bus to Calacalí, where local taxis travel to nearby Yunguilla. Alternatively, transfers can be arranged from Quito

EGYPT
ADRERE AMELLAL ECO LODGE

● *Stay in a Berber-style eco-lodge oozing traditional charm* ● *Discover architectural relics hidden in the desert oasis* ● *See traditional handicrafts from local artisans*

Escaping to Adrère Amellal is a special Egyptian experience, combining cultural charms and splendid scenery in a one-of-a-kind setting. As the country's first eco-lodge, it set an unprecedented standard for sustainable tourism in Egypt when it opened back in the '90s, and is still recognised as the best in class.

Built on the side of a towering limestone mountain, each of the fortress-like retreat's 40 rooms are made of *kershef* (a mixture of stone, salt water and a dozen different types of clay). In lieu of electricity, visitors use beeswax candles to light their way in the evenings.

The lodge also houses a handicrafts bazaar featuring typical wares made by the women of the oasis. Although not the typical luxury escape, Adrère Amellal undoubtedly offers a unique and unforgettable experience, with day trips into the desert included.

ON YOUR DOORSTEP
Tucked between the Qattara Depression and the Great Sand Sea in the Western Desert, the Siwa Oasis houses a bounty on ancient relics, from the 6th-century BC Temple of the Oracle to the 13th-century Fortress of Shali.

$ *Doubles incl meals/ activities USD$605*

🍽 *Egyptian cuisine*

Siwa Oasis; www. adrereamellal.net. From Cairo to Siwa (738km), book a private car transfer or take a West Delta Company bus

ETHIOPIA
COMMUNITY TREKS

● *Dive into Ethiopia's history and culture on a multi-day hike* ● *Visit ancient rock-hewn temples* ● *Bed down in homestays and community-run lodges*

With its nine Unesco World Heritage Sites, dramatic scenery and peerless history, it's no surprise Ethiopia has been drawing a growing number of tourists after years of being more strongly associated with political unrest and famine. With the nation recording the world's largest tourism growth in 2018, however, the importance of sustainable tourism has arguably never been greater.

Founded as a non-profit and now operating as Ethiopia's most prominent community tourism company, Tesfa Tours (whose name comes from Tourism in Ethiopia for Sustainable Future Alternatives) specialises in multi-day walking tours designed to empower local people to conserve their culture and protect the environment while delivering incredible guest experiences. Since developing its first routes in Lalibela and Tigray, both known for their ancient rock-hewn churches, Tesfa expanded to include walks in the rural villages within Simien National Park, and in the verdant forests of Wof Washa with wildlife species you won't see anywhere else on Earth. With each route planned in consultation with local communities to ensure it will bring sustainable benefits, this is trekking for good.

$ *Minimum 3-day community trek with Tesfa Tours (www.tesfatours.com) incl meals around US$70 per day*

🍽 *Traditional Ethiopian cuisine*

☞ **All four trekking areas are in the north. Tesfa Tours can assist with arranging transfers to the start**

FIJI
TANALOA TREKS

● *Learn about Fiji's history and culture on a local-guided hike* ● *Participate in a kava ceremony in a traditional highland village* ● *Eat and sleep in remote communities*

Few travellers to Fiji bother to explore beyond its (albeit lovely) beach resorts, but they're missing out, for the highlands of Viti Levu, the main island, don't just offer incredible hiking, but also myriad opportunities to gain a deeper insight into Fijian culture than you're likely to experience at typical coastal resort.

Working in partnership with local communities, Tanaloa Treks – Fiji's only dedicated hiking company – runs single and multi-day hikes designed to showcase the scenery and culture of the highlands in a culturally and environmentally responsible fashion. On the four-day cross-island hike, for example, you'll explore pristine forests, swim in cooling rivers, enjoy incredible vistas, and relax in remote villages where your guide grew up, for the company believes that the best people to lead trips are locals who know these lands best. Each day, your luggage will be driven ahead to the next village, where you'll stay and eat in simple homestays or locally managed lodges, which offer additional opportunities to connect with locals far from the tourist trail.

$ *4-day cross-island hike with Tanaloa Treks (https://tanaloa-treks-fiji) all-incl FJD$1100*

🍽 *Simple Fijian food*

☞ **Multi-day tours include pick-up from Suva and Suncoast hotels. Drop-off is usually in Nadi, but onward transfers are available**

FRENCH POLYNESIA
SUPPLY SHIP CRUISE IN THE MARQUESAS ISLANDS

● *Visit local villages in one of the most remote corners of the planet*
● *Explore archaeological sites or hike verdant jungles*

One of the most remote island groups in the world, the cinematically beautiful Marquesas Islands were once a major centre of Polynesian civilisation. Today, its inhabitants are guardians of the rich culture and traditions passed down by their ancestors. And while the islands have two domestic airports between them, an innovative cruise offers a surprisingly sustainable way to visit.

A hybrid freighter/passenger ship, the *Aranui 5* makes a 13-day supply run circuit around the islands from Tahiti every two-and-a-half weeks. Sleeping up to 254 passengers, the trip not only offers a rare taste of Marquesan life, but also a chance to visit parts of the island group that are virtually impossible to visit by other means. Spanning everything from visiting archaeological sites to tasting typical dishes in local restaurants to perhaps even taking in a local church service, the low-impact activity options at each of the dozen-odd stops provides a valuable income stream for locals.

Custom-built to replace the smaller *Aranui 3* in 2015, the ship is equipped with state-of-the-art technology designed to reduce its environmental impact (from a special smoke-cleaning system to LED lighting to water-saving showers). It also recycles all waste, desalinates seawater for use onboard, and trains staff to identify and fight against invasive species. Meals other than breakfast are cooked to order to prevent food waste, and the ship's owners have announced plans to replace plastic water bottles provided in the cabins with reusable water containers.

ON YOUR DOORSTEP
Back in Pape'ete, pick up a permit at the town hall (600CFP) and set out on the Fautaua Valley hike, which passes through verdant jungle and takes about three hours, including a stop at Fautaua Falls.

$ *13-day Aranui 5 cruise (www. aranui.com) all-incl from €4406*

⏺ *Accessible international dishes showcasing Polynesian fruit and vegetables*

☛ **The ship travels in a loop from Pape'ete, the capital of Tahiti**

GHANA

CASHEW VILLAGE LODGE

● Learn traditional weaving and drumming techniques ● Soak up the stories of village elders ● Learn the many uses of local trees on a guided village walk

The Volta River is the lifeblood of tiny Atsiekpoe ('home of the cashew tree') in southeastern Ghana, as visitors quickly learn when they arrive in the village by dugout canoe. Fishers repair boats and nets, children splash around and their mothers wash laundry at the riverside, where you will also find this Jolinaiko Eco Tours lodge, consisting of two typical thatched termite-clay buildings. It's a simple place with five bedrooms, a bucket shower and composting toilet, but it offers an opportunity to experience life in this remote fishing and farming village. Wander through Atsiekpoe (pronounced 'a-tjémpe') with a guide and learn the stories of a village elder, perhaps passing a weaver making baskets and mats from palm branches or a blacksmith producing iron tools. Guests can learn the locals' centuries-old trade secrets, whether it's weaving, hanging a river net between wooden poles to catch tilapia and shrimp, or Ewe drumming and dancing.

Jolinaiko ('jo-lin-eye-co') has another village lodge in neighbouring Togo, a B&B in Accra and offers tours to Benin and Burkina Faso, with the twofold aim of promoting cross-cultural exchanges and benefitting poor areas. Working with the Stepping Stones for Africa Foundation, the Ghanaian-Dutch operation has helped fund Atsiekpoe's electricity poles and wiring, as well as buy a motorised canoe and source building materials for the community latrines, tourist reception and museum. Tourist revenues now feed into a village fund for development projects, including improving sanitation and building a community centre.

ON YOUR DOORSTEP
Hike the lower Volta Region's coastal savannah landscape with an Atsiekpoe guide, or visit neighbouring villages by canoe. Further afield, walk to the 40m-high Wli Falls, catch some Hiplife music in Accra or cross the border to Togo's mountainous coffee-growing country around Kpalimé.

$ *Doubles half-board per person GHS80*

....

🍴 *Traditional local dishes and Volta River fish*

....

☛ *Atsiekpoe; www. joli-ecotours.com. From the capital Accra, head 90km east along the main coast road towards the Togolese border. Buses and shared taxis ply the route. Alternatively, hire a car with a local driver or book a Jolinaiko tour*

● **Community Interaction** ● **Arts & Traditions** ● **Homestays**

GUATEMALA
WEAVING VILLAGES JOURNEY

● *Tour village weaving and stitching co-ops off the tourist trail* ● *Learn traditional Guatemalan weaving techniques* ● *Stay in a mix of homestays and eco-hotels*

The Mesmoamerican region is famous for its textiles, from the colourful *huipiles* (long, sleeveless tunics) worn by local women to the intricately embroidered pillows and linens on display at artisan shops.

For travellers interested in learning more about the craftwork and cultural significance of these traditional designs, socially conscious Guatemalan operator Guate4You specialises in tours to communities where the nation's famously colourful textiles are woven. It works exclusively with local guides, homestays, restaurants, and artisans to ensure your money directly benefits the communities; it also supports a local weaving association to encourage the continued teaching of traditional arts.

Travellers with a particular passion for textiles should consider the eight-day weaving tour that visits Lake Atitlán, Quetzaltenango, and the Unesco-listed city of Antigua. Weaving experiences at every stop include demonstrations and lessons, as well as visits to weaving schools and opportunities to meet master weavers in remote communities.

$ *Guate4You (www. guate4you.com) weaving tours per day per person cost around US$250*

🍽 *Guatemalan*

☞ *All tours start at Guate4You's office in central Guatemala City*

INDIA

MAWLYNNONG VILLAGE

● *Stay in Khasi tribal homes in the cleanest village in India* ● *Learn life lessons from one of the world's few matrilineal societies* ● *Join locals in daily clean-ups*

Becoming the cleanest village in India takes some doing. The villagers of tiny Mawlynnong in Meghalaya started cleaning up their community after a cholera outbreak in colonial times, and today the whole village is involved, from the children who collect litter in conical bamboo baskets on their way to school to the farmers who volunteer as village gardeners, filling the lanes with tropical blooms. Everything organic is composted, plastic and smoking are banned, and non-biodegradable waste is taken away for proper disposal, leaving the streets looking, as locals describe it, like God's own country.

The enterprising people of Mawlynnong didn't stop at cleanliness. Women take a leading role in the matrilineal society of the Khasi tribe, and the village has 100% female literacy, compared to an India–wide average of 65%. Locals credit the women of Mawlynnong as the driving force that keeps the village looking spotless and serene.

Travellers who stay in the village's network of rustic homestays are invited to help out with the daily clean-up in between exploring the local jungle. Don't miss the handmade bamboo skyway climbing through the forest canopy, offering views over the edge of the plateau towards Bangladesh.

Sampling Khasi food is another treat. Ingredients are grown in the village's immaculate gardens, and evening meals include such delights as smoked banana flowers and *tungrymbai* (fermented soybeans with pork and black sesame). Needless to say, this is not your average India escape.

ON YOUR DOORSTEP
The most popular activity in Mawlynnong is trekking along tribal trails to living bridges woven from the roots of jungle trees. There's one just 15 minutes' walk from the village, and more scattered through the jungles surrounding Cherrapunjee.

$ *Doubles 1500-2500INR*

🍽 *Khasi tribal cuisine*

☞ *Pynursla, Vidhan Sabha, Meghalaya; www.mawlynnong. wordpress.com. Jeeps and long-distance buses run overland from Assam or Tripura to Cherrapunjee, where you can charter a waiting taxi to reach Mawlynnong. Alternatively, come uphill from Bangladesh via Dawki*

IRAN

AGHAMIR COTTAGE

● *Meet Iran's last nomads* ● *Eat at a restaurant empowering local women*
● *Spend the night in a heritage homestay* ● *Enjoy authentic Persian hospitality*

Ninety minutes' drive northeast of Shiraz, not far from the Unesco-listed ruins of Pasargadae, Aghamir Cottage is a homestay experience unlike any other in Iran.

After watching a TV programme on eco-lodge accommodation in Esfahan, Amir (Aghamir) Miri decided to transform his father's century-old cottage into a low-impact homestay for visitors to Pasargadae. Furnished with Persian rugs, with rooms opening into a sunny courtyard with a small fountain, the cosy homestay is a welcome retreat after a long day exploring the ruins. But it's more than just a homestay, with profits helping to fund everything from a campaign to protect Eurasian brown bears (which has led to the designation of a 1980 sq km no-hunting zone) to Bamad, a charming restaurant and handicrafts shop near Pasargadae's tomb of Cyrus the Great that provides local women with meaningful employment opportunities.

Passionate about preserving the culture of local Qashqai people (a confederation of five major nomadic tribes who camp in a valley beyond the ruins) Miri can also organise visits and even overnight stays with Qashqai families, with the idea that drawing awareness to their disappearing way of life may prove to be a catalyst for protecting it.

While it's possible to access Aghamir Cottage via public transport, it's easier to arrange a visit through a guide such as Sufi Tavafi (sufitavafi@gmail.com), a Tehran-based driver-guide with excellent English who has worked with Miri for years.

ON YOUR DOORSTEP

The ruins of Persepolis, an hour's drive south of Aghamir Cottage, might be more grand than those of Pasargadae, but with its well-preserved tomb thought to hold the remains of the founder of the first Persian Empire, Pasargadae's significance is nothing to be sniffed at.

$ *Homestay per person €30; Nomad stay per person €50*

🍽 *Traditional Persian cuisine included*

☞ *Sa'adat Shahr, Pasargad County, Fars Province; www.aghamir.ir. The cottage is located 21km south of Pasagarde, and is most easily visited with your own vehicle*

● **Community Interaction**   ● **Arts & Traditions**   ● **Homestays**

ITALY
LOCAL LIVING COASTAL TUSCANY TOUR

● *Stop and chat with locals off Italy's tourist trail* ● *Learn how to master traditional Tuscan dishes* ● *Stay in a traditional Tuscan home by the sea*

It's no secret that tourism has taken its toll on Italy, with the nation's ever-increasing volume of visitors blamed for everything from compromising quality of life for locals to turning cultural wonders into real-life amusement parks. Lucky, then, that responsible tourism champion G Adventures offers a range of small-group Local Living tours designed to connect travellers with a more authentic side of Italy without disrupting the local way of life in the destinations tours visit.

On the Coastal Tuscany tour, guests spend five nights in a traditional villa in the gorgeous (but largely unknown outside Italy)

medieval seaside town of Capalbio. Perfectly located for lazing on empty beaches, hiking amongst olive groves, visiting nearby villages and archaeological sites and soaking in hot springs, there are plenty of activities to keep you occupied. But arguably the best part of the experience is the opportunity it creates to connect more deeply with the destination and its people, including your local hosts. Did we mention there's lots of delicious home-cooking involved?

$ *6-night Coastal Tuscany tour with G Adventures (www.gadventures. com) CAD$2119*

▪◉▪ *Tuscan home cooking*

☞ **The tour begins and ends in Rome**

JAPAN

En-Ya Mt Fuji Ecotours

● *Meet locals in the untouristed foothills of Japan's highest peak* ● *Hike ancient Mt Fiji pilgrimage routes and visit a 300-year-old family-owned sake brewery*

'Conservation starts with community', says Masanori Shintani, an environmental scientist who set up En-Ya Mt Fuji Ecotours in 2017. Working on ecotourism projects in developing countries, he saw first-hand the importance of involving local people – and took that idea home to the small villages at the base of Japan's highest and most sacred mountain.

Day tours (from ¥11,000) range from hikes to bike rides led by local guides in Fuji's forested foothills and along quiet urban backroads. One trek follows part of the Muroyama Kodo, the oldest pilgrimage route up the mountain. Another joins the dots from village to village, stopping along the way to chat with local farmers, visit a sake brewery that's been in the same family since 1688, and enjoy a hearty soba noodle lunch in a small restaurant reducing food waste by using surplus produce from neighbouring farms.

Joining a tour not only creates employment and empowers communities to protect their natural surroundings – it offers the chance to connect with a simpler, healthier way of life. 'There are so many answers to life's problems in our villages,' says Shintani. From mid-2020, you'll also be able to sleep at the foot of Fuji in one of En-Ya's five new canvas bell tents pitched in a Japanese garden. The new glamping experience will include

$ *Glamping per night for two incl activities ¥60,000*

....

🍽 *Traditional Japanese with locally sourced ingredients*

....

☛ **Fujinomiya; www. mtfujiecotours.com. Fujinomiya is about 2 hours south-west of Tokyo by bullet train**

selected day tours as well as traditional local foods and farm and village tours, immersing you even more deeply in the real Japan.

ON YOUR DOORSTEP
If you're visiting between July and September, you can trek to the top of Mt Fuji from Fujinomiya, the shortest route. Also in Fujinomiya is the extraordinary Mt Fuji World Heritage Centre designed by Pritzker-winning architect Shigeru Ban.

JORDAN

FEYNAN ECOLODGE

● Enjoy authentic Bedouin hospitality while staying in off-grid luxury ● Explore the Dana Biosphere Reserve with a local guide ● Learn how to cook local specialities

Deep in the heart of Jordan's mountainous Dana Biosphere Reserve, a striking adobe lodge offers one of the most unique accommodation experiences on the planet.

Integrated with the local Bedouin community, Feynan Ecolodge treats guests to an authentic taste of traditional Bedouin life while providing locals with sustainable and meaningful employment opportunites, from working as lodge guides to making the candles that illuminate Feynan by night. More than just a place to stay, the lodge acts as a base for both outdoor exploration and cultural immersion, with the changing roster of daily (included) activities: everything from mountain biking to Roman ruins and hiking through rugged valleys in search of blue agama lizards to sampling cardamom-spiced coffee in a traditional goat-hair tent and learning the secret to cooking the perfect falafel.

Designed to minimise its impact on the reserve, the 26-room lodge is completely solar-powered, with single-use plastics avoided and water (sourced from a local spring) used sparingly. Comfort is not sacrificed for sustainability, however, with each individually designed guest room equipped with comfortable beds and hot showers. With produce sourced as locally as possible, delicious gourmet vegetarian meals are served on a shaded outdoor terrace dining area.

$ *Doubles all-incl from JOD170*

☞ **Feynan Ecolodge is a 3-hour drive from Amman, or 2 hours from Aqaba or Petra; www.ecohotels.me/ Feynan**

With so much to do at Feynan, it's the kind of place you should plan to stay for at least three nights, though no matter how long your visit, it never seems to feel long enough.

ON YOUR DOORSTEP
The lodge sits within striking distance of the Jordan Trail, a 600km-long hiking trail from the tip to tail of Jordan, established in 2015. From Feynan, it's a two-to-three-day hike along the trail to the ancient rock-cut city of Petra.

● **Community Interaction**   ● **Arts & Traditions**   ● **Homestays**

KENYA
Maji Moto Maasai Cultural Camp

● *Learn the stories behind Maasai beadwork from local artisans* ● *Sleep in a traditional Maasai warrior-style camp* ● *Discover the medicinal properties and spiritual significance of local plants*

A visit to a Maasai community can often feel like a show, but for real insight into the traditional Maasai way of life, head to this visionary community-owned camp, where profits pay for health, education and conservation efforts.

Set on an endless savannah east of the wildlife-rich Masai Mara National Reserve, there's accommodation to suit all budgets, from pitching your own tent and cooking your own food to catered cottages. Or for a taste of the warrior lifestyle, sleep under the stars at a remote bush camp (per person from US$150).

Walk through the Loita Hills with a long-limbed Maasai and discover their connection to the land – almost every plant is used for nutritional, medicinal or spiritual purposes. You might spot wildlife, from long-lashed giraffe to ostriches sprinting across the plain, and you'll definitely meet herders tending their livestock, the economic mainstay of these pastoralist peoples.

Or visit the widows' village to see what they cook (perhaps roasted goat or vegetable stew) and how they create their colourful beadwork. And as night falls, sit around the campfire to a soundtrack of Maasai songs and stories.

$ *Tent incl activities US$20 per person*

🍽 *Traditional Kenyan*

☞ *Narok; http:// majimotomaasai camp.com. The camp can arrange transfers from Nairobi (3-4 hours), and pickups from Narok bus stop*

LESOTHO
Malealea Lodge

● Get a feel for village life on a local-guided walk ● Hike to ancient rock art sites created by Africa's first peoples ● Learn more about local life at a homestay

If you only visit one place in Lesotho, a tiny high-altitude kingdom encircled by South Africa, make it Malealea Lodge. First established as a trading post in 1905 before being transformed into visitor accommodation by its current Lesotho-born owners, the charming 74-room lodge in the nation's southwest offers the opportunity to experience local culture and outdoor activities in the one spot, with every visit helping to support the local community.

High on the agenda of lodge activities, led by local guides, is a pony-trek or hike to a centuries-old San rock art site, while the village walk typically includes an eye-opening visit to the very traditional local brewery. Every sunset, village choirs and bands perform for guests before a hearty braai dinner is dished up by the village chief's wife.

Constantly improving the sustainability of the lodge, which offers sleeping options ranging from camping to characterful thatched-roof rondavel huts, the Jones family switched from generator power to solar in 2016, and have developed a natural sewage system to help limit its impact in light of Lesotho's ongoing struggle with land degradation caused primarily by destructive agricultural practices. Guests are encouraged to refill their own water bottles with spring water provided, and while lodge profits support the humanitarian work of the Maleala Development trust, there are also locally made handicrafts for sale from the village's small boutique.

ON YOUR DOORSTEP
Visitors keen to learn more about local culture, politics and Basotho life can opt for a homestay in the adjoining village with the likes of Ntate David Mokala (half of Lesotho's almost-Olympic equestrian team) and his wife Me Manthabiseng.

$ *Doubles from ZAR240*

International favourites with a Basotho twist

☛ *Malealea Village, Mafeteng district; www.malealea.com. The lodge lies 700km west of Durban in South Africa. You'll need your own wheels, or join a tour that visits the lodge*

How to choose a responsible tour operator

There's no denying that planning a sustainable trip can take a bit of legwork, particularly for travel to remote destinations and developing countries. So why not recruit an operator to do it for you?

'By travelling with a tour operator that's genuinely committed to operating responsibly, the fundamentals of supporting local communities and limiting your environmental footprint will have already been built in to your trip,' says James Thornton, CEO of small-group tour company Intrepid Travel, known for its pioneering responsible tourism strategies.

If you prefer to travel independently, chances are you will still use operators for short excursions along the way. Here's how to ensure those you travel with will help to minimise your footprint on your destination.

WHAT DOES IT MEAN TO TRAVEL RESPONSIBLY?

'Travelling responsibly is about demonstrating respect for the people, culture and environment you're visiting,' says Thornton. Responsible (and in effect, sustainable) travel also helps to fund environmental and cultural conservation and gives locals a reason to conserve.

'When you take a responsible holiday you are ensuring that the money you spend benefits the local community,' says Justin Francis, CEO of UK-based travel company Responsible Travel, which sells tours from 400 specialist operators around the world. 'This might mean staying in a family-owned lodge instead of a multinational chain, discovering local eateries that celebrate local cuisine as part of their culture, or going kayaking with a local guide.'

IS RESPONSIBLE AND SUSTAINABLE TOURISM POSSIBLE EVERYWHERE?

While travelling to countries that your own government forbids (typically for safety reasons), is not generally considered responsible, due in part to the strain it can put on local services, industry experts claim responsible and sustainable travel is possible in places with poor ethical records.

'Travelling responsibly is less about the destination but more about what you do when you get there,' says Francis. 'It's possible to travel in an extremely damaging way in countries with even the greatest commitments to human rights and the environment.'

Kelly Galaski, Director of Global Programs for the Planeterra Foundation, the not-for-profit partner of small-group tour company G Adventures, agrees.

'By experiencing different places and cultures in the most responsible way possible, travellers can become advocates for bettering our world when they return to their home countries,' she says. 'Responsible travel operators are crucial in connecting travellers to business owners that are creating opportunities for many at the grassroots level.'

IDENTIFYING RESPONSIBLE TRAVEL OPERATORS

In recent years, many operators have overhauled their offerings to ensure they are more responsible and sustainable. Checking the operator's website for a responsible or sustainable tourism policy is the easiest way to assess its credentials.

These policies typically reflect the World Tourism Organization's definition of sustainable tourism, and may incorporate additional measures based on the company's own research, or that of non-governmental organisations and academic bodies. Since removing elephants rides from its tours, for example, Intrepid Travel has taken measures to secure the safety of vulnerable children in communities it visits.

'We want to create the best possible experiences for our travellers while ensuring the places we visit are impacted positively,' says Thornton. 'That's why instead of including visits to schools or orphanages which pose risks to children, we'll eat and shop at social enterprise restaurants and stores whose earnings fund programs to help keep families together.'

Sustainable tourism certification is also increasing, as are sustainable tour aggregators like Responsible Travel, which vets the tours it sells against its own strict criteria.

KEY INGREDIENTS OF A RESPONSIBLE TOUR

- Low-impact wildlife experiences such as viewing wildife in the wild, and visits to legitimate wildlife sanctuaries.

- Cultural visits that benefit local communities first, and visitors second.

- Community tourism that keeps children safe and families together (read: no orphanage visits or experiences that support child labour).

- Accommodation in homestays and boutique properties.

- Dining experiences based around seasonal local produce, local cultural traditions, and local-owned establishments.

- Local guides that are appropriately trained, outfitted and paid for the services they provide.

- Waste-minimising initiatives such as offering clients reusable alternatives to common single-use plastics like carry bags and water bottles.

MONGOLIA
LIVING WITH NOMADS

● *Tend livestock belonging to Mongolian nomads* ● *Learn to make dried curds and fermented mare's milk* ● *Share meals with locals and stay overnight in a traditional ger*

Camping in the wild takes on a whole other dimension in Mongolia where nomadic life has been practiced for millennia. Living in *ger*, large circular canvas tents that can be dismantled in less than an hour, herder families are fully mobile in their search for grasslands to feed their animals. It's a tough and demanding life, but one that continues to appeal to Mongolians who enjoy the freedom, independence and connection to nature that it provides.

In recent years, nomadic families have started hosting travellers who wish to experience this nomadic lifestyle – it provides an additional income stream to cover lean times and an incentive to keep up their traditions. Several local operators include horseback, camel or yak riding in such tour packages. Truth be told, though, if you're not experienced at travelling on the back of an animal, it can leave you feeling saddle sore.

A great alternative is Stone Horse Expeditions & Travel's Train to Ger trips, which can be combined with Trans-Siberian railway journeys. You'll be driven out of Ulaanbaatar to join your hosts in the rolling countryside of Darkhid valley. Staying either with the family in their cosy *ger* or in a *ger* of your own, you'll share meals that include foods made from the milk of their livestock. Stone Horse Expeditions take seriously the protection of the environment, and treat fairly the herder families they work with on their tours.

ON YOUR DOORSTEP
In Ulaanbaatar you'll find traditional handicrafts at fair trade Mary & Martha Mongolia (www.mmmongolia.com); the Mongolian Quilting Shop (www.dragonflyquilts.com/mongolia.htm), which sells handmade quilts produced by low-income families; and the non-profit Tsagaan Alt Wool Shop (www.mongolianwoolcraft.com).

$ *2 night ger/1 night city guesthouse tour with Stone Horse Expedition & Travel (www.stonehorsemongolia.com) US$295*

🍽 *Mongolian nomad staples, including milk products and mutton*

☛ *Rates incl local transport from Ulaanbaatar to Darkhid Valley (90 minutes' drive)*

MONGOLIAN HOMESTAY ETIQUETTE

Demonstrating respect for Mongolian customs is crucial for a memorable *ger* (Mongolian tent) stay. Key etiquette tips include bringing a small gift, always receiving objects with your right hand, never refusing food and drink (just take a nibble if you're not hungry), and keeping your arms and wrists covered. And resist the urge to try on the hat!

MOROCCO
TOUDA ECO LODGE

● Join guesthouse staff for singing and traditional dancing after dinner ● Visit nomadic families in the local mountains ● Buy locally woven crafts in Bougmez Valley villages

More like a large family gathering where everyone is warmly welcomed, Touda Eco Lodge is comfortable but modest, as is everything about staying here. The rooms are sparingly decorated with local handmade rugs; the hot water is solar heated; and electricity is used sparingly. All the materials – stone, wood and mud – used to build the lodge are from here. Cars are a rare sight, as villagers walk or ride horses and mules to get around. The only sounds floating up from the valley are of the wind in the trees, children playing and birdsong.

In the quiet lounge, coffee table books celebrate the culture and nomadic people of the High Atlas, who have lived here in harmony with the landscape for millennia. Meals are lovingly prepared each day by staff from the village and consumed either outside, with dramatic views of mountains, or inside together with other guests drawn to the lounge and fireplace after dinner.

ON YOUR DOORSTEP
Take a horse trek across the mountains to visit nomadic families and share a meal, before joining in the afternoon siesta in their temporary camp. Communal living here sees everything shared.

$ *Doubles from €30*

🍽 *Locally sourced traditional Berber dishes*

☛ *Ait Bougmez; www. touda.co.uk*

MYANMAR
INLE HERITAGE

● Sleep in traditional-style stilt houses with solar-powered showers ● See quality souvenirs handcrafted by local artisans ● Take an Ithar cooking class with a local chef

Central Myanmar's Unesco-listed Inle Lake has been described as an ecosystem fighting to survive, which makes the work of Inle Heritage – a non-profit designed to preserve the lake's nature and culture – all the more important. This work is funded by visitors who enjoy sleeping in Inle Heritage's luxury stilt-house accommodation, sampling well executed traditional dishes in its restaurant, browsing artisanal handicrafts in its gift shop and gallery, and participating in Inthar cooking classes using local ingredients.

Despite a fabulous sense of calm at Inle Heritage, there's always much ado at the property, which includes a Burmese cat-breeding centre and an endemic fish aquarium (which guests can visit) and a vocational training school for locals, all with an eye toward teaching conservation and sustainability to new generations.

ON YOUR DOORSTEP
The hotel is at the southern end of Inle; the adjacent village of Inn Paw Khon is home to traditional craft and lotus silk weaving centres. Tours of the workshops can be arranged through Inle Heritage, with products for sale directly benefiting the artisans.

$ *Doubles from $150*

🍽 *Modern Inthar food*

☛ *Inn Paw Khon Village, Inle Lake, Shan State; www. inleheritage.org. The hotel is an hour by boat from Nyaungshwe, from where you can arrange boat taxis*

MYANMAR

MYAING COMMUNITY TOURISM PROJECT

● *Visit the nation's first community tourism project* ● *Enjoy traditional meals prepared by a local women's collective* ● *Discover the secret behind Myanmar's natural cosmetic paste*

Community-based tourism is still an emerging concept in Myanmar. But the nation's first – and currently only – offering might just be one of the most memorable experiences you enjoy in the country.

Developed in partnership with international NGO ActionAid and Intrepid Travel, the project is located in the township of Myaing, one of the poorest and least developed regions of Myanmar. Benefiting more than 1150 community members living in a cluster of four villages, the typical two-night program includes visits to all four villages, with visits structured to provide hosts and guests unique opportunities for cultural exchange in each village. While you might help to plant fruit trees in one village, you could have a traditional beauty treatment called 'thanaka' applied in another. At the end of the day, you'll bed down at a basic but comfortable traditional-style community lodge nearby.

Prepared by the local women-led Self Help Group, designed to empower rural women to take more active roles in society, meals served during the experience are some of the most traditional (and tasty) you'll

sample in Myanmar. The lodge also provides employment opportunities for locals, from cleaning to serving customers in its souvenir shop packed with locally-made trinkets. With visits initially restricted to Intrepid tours while the project found its feet, visits are now also possible with a handful of other operators.

ON YOUR DOORSTEP

The villages of Myaing offer an authentic slice of Myanmarese life that only a fraction of international travellers have the privilege to experience. Enjoy the opportunity to soak up traditional hospitality, being sure to ask permission before photographing locals.

$ *15-day Best of Myanmar tour with Intrepid Travel (www.intrepid. com) AU$2700*

....

🍽 *Hearty, traditional meat and vegetable dishes with rice*

....

☛ **The community tourism project in Myaing, less than 2 hours' drive north of Bagan, is most easily visited on Intrepid Travel's Best of Myanmar tour**

NAMIBIA
Ju/'Hoansi Living Museum

● *Meet the descendants of Africa's first peoples* ● *Learn how the San people have lived in harmony with the natural environment for centuries*

Known for their short stature and distinctive 'clicking' language, the San are thought to be the first inhabitants of southern Africa, where they've lived for millennia as semi-nomadic hunter-gatherers. Removed from their traditional hunting grounds and subjected to various government-mandated modernisation programmes over the years, a mere 2000 of the estimated 30,000 San living in Namibia are thought to maintain their traditional lifestyle. But thanks to a clutch of living museums, the nation's last San people are being empowered to prevent their ancient traditions from becoming lost.

Initiated by a Namibian tour guide and a teacher from Grashoek, a San village in Nambia's remote northwest, the Ju/'Hoansi Living Museum has been run by the local community since it opened in 2004. The successful sustainable tourism model has since been adopted by five other San communities around the country.

While most visitors spend just a few hours at the terrific museum – where the local San community demonstrate traditional techniques explained by an excellent guide – you can also opt for a three-day experience during

which you'll learn how to make San equipment to use in the bush, make your own sleeping shelter, and forage for your own food. You'll even get to visit your host family in the modern village to see how San people live today. With all programmes possible upon arrival at the museum, which is open 365 days a year, you don't even need to book ahead.

ON YOUR DOORSTEP
You can also opt to stay at the basic camping area behind the museum for NAD$50 per person per night (BYO food). For more comfort, the excellent Roy's Rest Camp lies 80km west of the museum. There's not much else around for miles.

$ *3 day Ju/'Hoansi experience NAD$750*

⏐○⏐ *Simple southern African staples*

☛ Grashoek; www. lcfn.info/juhoansi. The museum and campsite is 2 hours northeast of Grootfontein, next to the San village of Grashoek, 7km north of the C44

NEPAL
Tamang Heritage &
Langtang Valley Trek

● *Interact with Tamang people while trekking through remote mountain villages* ● *Stay with families in small locally owned teahouses*

Women wearing traditional tunic-like dresses and felt hats stand at the doorways of their stone houses. Men look up from heavy loads of firewood on their backs. Children pause their play to chirp 'namaste' as you pass.

The seldom-visited Tamang Heritage Trail, a six-day loop trail on the western edge of Langtang National Park, north of Kathmandu, might be riddled with mountain views, but unlike more popular Himalayan treks it passes through remote culturally Tibetan Tamang villages where daily life has changed little in the centuries.

It's a low-altitude trek by Nepal standards; the highest point is a 3100m-high alpine meadow you reach on day five. But the terrain is steep; you're never far from stone steps or switchbacks. The upside is seeing drone-like vistas as you climb – of villages such as Gatlang and Thuman and snowy ranges such as Ganesh Himal, which straddles the Tibetan border. Trek in spring and you'll see Nepal's ridiculously pretty rhododendrons in bloom – enormous trees dotted all over with pink, snow-white and rose-red posies – and maybe a few black-faced langur monkeys.

By staying in basic family-owned teahouses built for traders rather than tourists, and enjoying Nepali fare such as momos (Nepalese dumplings) and daal bhaat (rice, lentil soup and curry), you're providing an income for Tamang communities off the tourist trail that were badly affected by Nepal's devastating 2015 earthquakes.

An easy traverse on day seven of the trek offered by sustainable travel pioneer Intrepid Travel connects you with the gentler and more scenic Langtang Valley Trek, which also suffered considerable earthquake damage. Two treks in one and the opportunity to have a positive effect on local people? Just say yes.

$ *Intrepid Travel (www.intrepidtravel.com) combines both trails on a 15-day trek, incl transport, accommodation and some meals for AUD$1545*

🍽 *Traditional Nepalese*

☛ **Tours begin and end in Kathmandu, Nepal's capital**

PANAMA

ARTISANAL IMMERSION

● *Discover Panamanian culture through arts and crafts* ● *Meet expert artisans and learn from their mastery* ● *Paint your own ceramic plate or tile with precolonial motifs*

Cultural exchange is fundamental to responsible travel. However, independent travellers sometimes struggle to make connections with locals, especially when there are linguistic barriers. Tour operator EcoCircuitos Panama helps bridge this chasm through mindfully crafted experiences such as its Artisanal Panama tour, a dive into the country's diverse, colourful and too-often-unseen art scene.

In keeping with EcoCircuitos' hands-on approach to travel, this tour motivates visitors to directly experience a different side of Panama – to learn basket-weaving from the Emberá, one of the country's seven indigenous cultures; take painting classes with Afro-Panamanian community members in the laid-back Caribbean fishing village of Portobello; meet with young talent in a creative space in Casco Antiguo, the historic old quarter of Panama City; and learn about making pottery, masks and *polleras* (large embroidered skirts that are the national dress of Panama) in villages of the Azuero Peninsula, the heart of Spanish colonial culture in Panama and birthplace of Panamanian folklore and tradition.

But the tours are also for the artists who are empowered to see the value of their trades and continue pursuing them, thus conserving Panamanian heritage. Any purchase of local arts and crafts directly benefits artisans and helps to sustain their communities.

Environmental sustainability is not forgotten, either. On Isla Gobernadora, for example, a special 'art lodge' supports a community art cooperative and, for visitors, organises workshops that connect creativity with environmental stewardship. Along the way, meal stops give prominence to Panama's local cuisine infused with the flavours of fresh local produce, seafood and other unique ingredients.

$ *10-day artisanal tour with EcoCircuitos (www.ecocircuitos. com) USD$1995*

....

IOI *Typical Panamanian cuisine in local restaurants*

....

☛ *Panama City's Tocumen International Airport is the departure point for this tour*

PERU

SACRED VALLEY & LARES ADVENTURE

● Visit mountain communities off the tourist trail ● Enjoy a traditional weaving demonstration in an alpine village virtually untouched by tourism ● Explore some of Peru's lesser-known Inca ruins

If there's a silver lining to the ever-increasing flow of tourists to Machu Picchu, it's the alternative pathways to Peru's most famous Inca site that have been devised to help lessen the impact. Beginning near the village of Lares, the three-day, two-night Lares trail is a great option for hikers keen to escape the crowds. But with most people choosing to camp along the route, which has little tourism infrastructure, the benefit to locals can be minimal.

Owned by Peruvians with a passion for Andean culture, Mountain Lodges of Peru's Sacred Valley and Lares Adventure is designed to sustain local communities while simultaneously minimising your environmental footprint. Combining visits to key Sacred Valley Inca sites and the most interesting hiking sections of the Lares Trail, the tour can be completed in five or seven days. En route, guests stay in luxurious, low-impact lodges constructed in consultation with local communities. Locals are not only provided with the hospitality

training necessary to join lodge personnel teams, but are also investors in the properties. The tour includes exclusive experiences ranging from a traditional lunch prepared by a farming village that previously reaped no benefit from tourism in the area, to a visit to a traditional weaving community beyond the beaten path.

Led by a highly trained Peruvian guide, the expedition is topped off with a visit to Machu Picchu on the final day before heading back to Cuzco.

ON YOUR DOORSTEP
Check out the Centro de Textiles Tradicionales del Cuzco (textilescusco.org), a not-for-profit set up to support Andean weavers, which also has a small on-site museum.

$ *5-day tour with Mountain Lodges of Peru (mountainlodges ofperu.com) all-incl US$1899*

────────

❮❮❮❮ *Gourmet international dishes crafted with local produce*

────────

☛ Fujinomiya; www. mtfujiecotours.com. Tours depart from and return to the city of Cuzco in Peru's Sacred Valley

---

TACKLING OVERTOURISM AT MACHU PICCHU

The ever-increasing popularity of Machu Picchu prompted authorities to add another layer of ticket restrictions in 2019 to help protect the Inca site, with visitors now required to choose from one of three circuits (Circuit 1 is the most comprehensive) in a one-way direction. Once you make your choice, you must stick with it.

SWEDEN

GEUNJA SAMI ECO LODGE

● *Hike through Swedish Lapland with a Sami guide* ● *Learn indigenous Sami wisdom and relish in fireside storytelling* ● *Discover the many uses of local herbs*

To visit the Geunja Sami Eco Lodge is to completely disconnect from the modern world and travel back to a simpler time when there was no electricity, wi-fi or social media. This low-impact operation (which only welcomes guests 12 times per year) invites visitors to instead learn some bushcraft skills, study medicinal herbs, take a dip in the lake, light up the wood-burning sauna, fish for dinner and forage for cloudberries and chanterelles in the surrounding forests. Think of it like a digital detox with an ancestral twist.

Reindeer herder Mikael Vinka and his Sami family will regale you with local wisdom, traditions and legends of Swedish Lapland over a billowing bonfire in the *goathie* (a type of teepee used by Sami for millennia). You can also join Vinka on a trek following his ancestor's footprints into the nearby Vindel Mountains, where it's possible to learn about the conservation work he does with the Swedish government to protect the arctic fox.

There are – appropriately – no roads connecting Geunja with the outside world; access is via boat. You sleep either on a bed

of reindeer hides in the *goathie* or under the orange glow of a kerosene lamp in a shared timber cabin with six beds. A crackling fire ensures you survive the crisp Lapland night and wake up fresh for more Sami-inspired detoxing.

ON YOUR DOORSTEP
Ammarnäs lies near the southern end of the famed Kungsleden (King's Trail), a 440km hut-to-hut hiking route through Sweden's far north. The path traverses varied landscapes of the Lapland mountain world from low-lying birch forests to craggy alpine plateaus.

$ *3-day tour per person all-incl from SEK13,900*

|●| *Traditional Sami meals with fresh and foraged ingredients*

☛ **Ammarnäs; www. bjorkexperience.com. The boat ride from Ammarnäs to the eco-lodge is included in the rate**

TIMOR-LESTE
ECO-DISCOVERY TIMOR-LESTE

● *Connect with communities off the beaten path* ● *Tour traditional dwellings and bed down in a conical Bunak house*

It's one of Australia's closest neighbours, but despite having a culture as rich as the biodiverse coral reefs that fringe it, Timor-Leste still ranks among the world's least-visited countries more than 20 years on from its fight for independence. High prices (by Southeast Asian standards) and a lack of tourism infrastructure beyond Dili are the main culprits, but if you can get past that,

this now-peaceful nation offers one of the most fascinating travel experiences on the planet.

While it's not a large country, Timor-Leste's diabolical roads and unreliable public transport add additional levels of difficulty to exploring beyond Dili. Run by passionate locals, Eco-Discovery Timor-Leste offers the perfect solution: tailor-made tours of the country led by local guides who speak English, Portuguese and Tetum (the official languages), as well as Indonesian and a number of other local dialects, offering travellers an opportunity to connect more deeply with locals you meet along the way. From jungle hideouts used by Fretilin resistance fighters during the Indonesian occupation to incredible cultural relics that have miraculously survived to this day, Eco-Discovery can take you there in a culturally and environmentally responsible manner, supporting community-based projects and businesses en route. And with every dollar you spend staying in the country, you'll play a role in helping to rebuild it.

ON YOUR DOORSTEP
Kick off your visit to the country with a Dili History Tour (jdntimorleste.weebly.com). Run by Timorese students, tours cover the story of Timor-Leste's independence, travelling around to various historical sites in the capital by *mikrolet* (small mini-van).

$ *Tailor-made tours per day all-incl per person around US$100*

🍽 *Simple but hearty Timorese dishes*

☛ *Landmark Plaza, Dili; www. ecodiscovery-easttimor.com*

UZBEKISTAN
VILLAGE-TO-VILLAGE HIKING

● *Meet locals in small Central Asian mountain communities* ● *Take in traditional musical performances and visit ancient petroglyphs* ● *Sleep in rural homes owned by locals*

Tucked up in Uzbekistan's Nuatau Mountains and dating back to the time of Alexander the Great lies the Tajik village of Sentyab (Sentob). Built largely out of stone, the remote village is the starting point for local operator Responsible Travel's seven-day village-to-village trek. The ultimate active cultural immersion for intrepid travellers, the guided trip will see hikers picnic near remote lake Aydarkul, visit archaeological sites including ancient petroglyphs and the ruins of a Mongol fortress, eat traditional meals with rural mountain families – reputed to be among the nation's friendliest people – and watch local artisans at work, though you can expect to be encouraged to try your own hand at weaving and other skills.

The Uzbek-owned tour operator's business model is designed to attract international travellers to the country's outdoor offerings and prove to locals that environmental tourism and protection leads to economic stability. By booking directly with Responsible Travel (which offers a range of community-based tours in the mountains), you're ensuring that your tourism dollars are benefiting the people of the Tajik, Kazakh and Uzbek villages you'll be visiting.

Each night of the tour, which includes out-and-back hikes as well as point-to-point travel, you'll bed down at simple homestays. But while luxuries beyond Western-style toilets are minimal, you can expect hosts eager to fatten you up on traditional dishes made with locally grown produce. There's usually also plenty of time between the treks to wander around the surprisingly diverse villages. Keep an eye out for desert monitors, wild boars, and even wolves, all of which you might spot in various forests along the trek.

$ *7-day trek with Responsible Travel (www.nuratau.com) incl meals per person from US$280*

....

🍽 *Traditional Uzbek cuisine*

....

☞ *The tour starts at the Responsible Travel Office in Bog'don (Yangiqishloq)*

VIETNAM
DA BAC COMMUNITY-
BASED TOURISM

● *Stay in a stilt house and support a village devoted to preserving its culture* ● *Experience traditional therapies handed down through generations* ● *Experience village life far from the tourist crowds*

Tribal tourism has lured travelers to the hills of Vietnam since the country first opened up to outsiders, but it hasn't always been done with the best interests of tribal people at heart. Learning lessons from the armies of backpackers storming the hills around Sapa, the villagers of Da Bac established their own model for tourism on a micro-scale, with local people involved at every stage of the process.

Today, a string of families from the Dao Tien and Muong Ao Ta tribes have transformed their wooden village stilt homes into simple homestays, after travelling around Vietnam to learn the ropes from other homestay programmes. The extra revenue raised helps supplement earnings from fishing and farming and subsidising community initiatives, such as lessons for children in vanishing tribal languages and traditional song and dance.

Guests are often invited to help out on the farms or in the kitchen when not exploring the surrounding valleys by bike, kayak or on foot. There are no must-see sights, but that's rather the point; travel here is about leaving behind modern notions and immersing yourself in a different way of life. In Da Bac, this means sleeping under a mosquito net on a mattress on the floor, and learning to communicate non-verbally with families whose friendly hospitality exceeds their English-language skills, with the perk of fine country cooking and traditional herbal baths.

ON YOUR DOORSTEP
Exploring the countryside is part of the Da Bac experience, and bikes and kayaks are rented out for rural roaming. Village guides can lead trekkers to rice terrace viewpoints, forest streams and hidden caverns in the jungle.

$ *Doubles VND100,000*

🍽 *Traditional Vietnamese village cuisine*

☞ *Da Bac Village, Hoa Binh Province; www.dabaccbt.com. The homestays of Da Bac CBT are dotted around the countryside near Da Bac township, west of Hanoi*

● **Community Interaction** ● **Arts & Traditions** ● **Homestays**

VIETNAM
SU LINH TREKKING

● *Meet locals in a traditional Hmong village* ● *Learn Hmong weaving and cooking* ● *Stay with your host's family in Lo Chai*

A sprawling region of tiered rice fields in the Hoang Lien Son mountains near the Vietnam–China border, Sapa has been a popular trekking base for international tourists for decades. So popular, that tourism has been blamed for threatening the way of life for locals, many of whom do not benefit from the revenue it generates. By booking a trek through Su Linh, you can be sure it does. Though Su, who is from the Hmong ethnic group, has never left Sapa, she's taught herself English, as well as several other languages, from guiding tourists. On an overnight trek, you'll stay at her aunt's home in the town of Lo Chai. Though accommodation is simple – mattresses on the floor with quilts and mosquito nets – it's quite comfortable and Su will ensure an authentic experience: you'll be able to try your hand at weaving, and cook with the family; meals are included in the price of the treks. The best part? The cost of the excursion goes to Su Linh's family and surrounding villages.

$ *2-night trek per person from US$70*

🍽 *Hmong cuisine*

☛ **Pickups from Sapa hotels; www. sulinhsapatrekking. wordpress.com. You can take the overnight Hanoi–Lo Cai train, then a bus to Sapa (40 minutes)**

- Eco-luxury
- Sustainable Dining
- Community Interaction

URBAN

● Eco-luxury   ● Sustainable Dining   ● Community Interaction

ARGENTINA

HOME HOTEL

● *Bed down in Buenos Aires' first 'green' hotel* ● *Sample homemade cakes in the lush garden* ● *Mingle with locals at the popular on-site bar*

Tucked behind an unassuming vine-covered building in the buzzy barrio of Palermo Hollywood, Home was arguably Buenos Aires' first eco-conscious hotel. Still among the city's top boutique choices more than a decade on, the chic but refreshingly unpretentious hotel feels more like a mid-century home.

Decorated with vintage floral wallpaper and llama blankets, Home's 20 guest rooms – ranging from cosy doubles to a spacious poolside suite with an outdoor fireplace – echo the homely vibe, with eco-friendly initiatives ranging from toiletries provided in reusable dispensers to room keys that power down the rooms when not in use.

Just off the lobby, the in-house restaurant showcases seasonal local produce in its excellent continental breakfast buffet and accessible a la carte lunch and dinner offerings. Doubling as a bar in the evening, the sun-drenched space spills out into an urban oasis brimming with native trees. There's even a small solar-heated pool (open October to March) in the garden, with free sauna access for guests in the hotel's small spa.

Home works with local community groups to recycle glass, plastic and cardboard (Argentina doesn't have an official recycling programme), and dispose of batteries safely. Worn towels, sheets and slippers are donated to charity groups working with children and the elderly, while kitchen oils are handed over to the city for the manufacture of biofuels. Add some of the city's most helpful hotel staff, and it's no wonder Home's popularity endures.

ON YOUR DOORSTEP

Home is just steps from some of Palermo's trendiest boutiques, restaurants and bars; local-approved recommendations are provided in the complimentary Home guide. Don't miss the Mercado de las Pulgas flea market, just three blocks west.

$ *Doubles from US$130*

 Contemporary international fare

☛ **Palermo Hollywood, Buenos Aires; www.home buenosaires.com**

● **Eco-luxury** ● **Sustainable Dining** ● **Community Interaction**

above & following page: Alex Hotel

AUSTRALIA
ALEX HOTEL

● *Lap up luxe plastic-free amenities* ● *Slumber in minimalist comfort* ● *Hang out with locals in the lobby cafe and bar* ● *Go on, order the Shark Bay crab pasta*

Entering this boutique hotel in Perth's cultural heart, you might think you've stumbled into a cool cafe. But this was the intention of its owners (of Little Creatures craft beer fame) who designed the 74-room hotel to feel more like a home away from home.

The minimalist, pastel-toned rooms are designed as spaces to dream, and guests are encouraged to relax in three chic communal living areas. With typical in-room amenities provided in the mezzanine-level lounge, the approach creates a great social vibe, and goes a long way to lower the hotel's impact. But it doesn't stop there, with bathroom products by natural Australian skincare brand Sodashi provided in reusable dispensers, and drinking water bottled on site. In-room movies are free, and you can order excellent Italian-inspired room service from the next-door Shadow Wine Bar & Dining Room, which champions Western Australian produce.

ON YOUR DOORSTEP

Set in the revived inner-city suburb of Northbridge, the Alex is close to some of Perth's best cafes, restaurants and bars, as well as cultural attractions such as the Art Gallery of WA, Western Australian Museum and State Theatre Centre.

$ *Doubles from AUD$200*

🍽 *Plastic-free home-made breakfast*

☛ **50 James St, Perth; www.alexhotel. com.au**

● Eco-luxury   ● Sustainable Dining

AUSTRIA
BOUTIQUE HOTEL STADHALLE

● *Drizzle your organic breakfast cereal with honey from the on-site apiary*
● *Opt for a room with views of Vienna's largest lavender garden*

Many hotels make bold claims when it comes to sustainability, but Vienna's Boutique Hotel Stadthalle has the chops to make a case for its own claim to being the world's first zero-energy balance urban hotel, which means it creates as much energy as is needed to power it, mostly via a massive solar panel installation, though wind turbines are also on the way. It's easy to forget how green the hotel is, though, when you're staying in one of its comfortable 76 rooms. Some have views over the hotel's rooftop lavender garden, and while the prices are already reasonable, there's a 10% discount if you arrive by bike or public transport. If you plan to explore Vienna on bike, be sure to start your day with breakfast in the hotel's organic garden, complete with honey sourced from its on-site apiary.

ON YOUR DOORSTEP
Boutique Hotel Stadthalle lies only a block from the shops on Mariahilfer Strasse. Check out Greenground (greenground.at) for modern sustainable clothing and Zerum for fair-trade EU-produced products (zerum.at).

$ *Doubles from €88*

⦿| *Organic Viennese continental breakfast*

☛ **Hackengasse 20, Vienna; www. hotelstadthalle. at. The hotel is a 5-minute walk from Westbahnhof U-Bahn**

CAMBODIA

Jaya House Riverpark

● Stay in luxe plastic-free rooms showcasing local artwork ● Dine on contemporary organic Cambodian cuisine ● Enjoy eco-friendly amenities like reusable water bottles and paper coffee pods

Set on a tranquil stretch of Siem Reap's leafy riverfront, one of Asia's first plastic-free hotels mixes style with a social conscience. Jaya House Riverpark's architecture was inspired by 1960s Cambodian modernism with interiors crafted from sustainably sourced wood and local stone. And it showcases the work of the city's talented artisans, including paintings commissioned from the city's Small Art School, which gives free art classes to underprivileged children, one of four NGOs the boutique hotel supports.

Spacious, neutral-toned rooms and suites come with supremely comfortable beds and a balcony or terrace overlooking the tropical garden, while eco-friendly details include laundry baskets made by Rehash Trash (a local recycling-orientated social enterprise) and a coffee machine with paper pods. You even get your own water bottle – the hotel co-launched the ReFillNotLandfill initiative, now in 10 countries and counting.

There's also a wheelchair-accessible tuk-tuk that can whisk you around the city, and tours to take you temple- or gallery-hopping, birdwatching, kayaking and more. When not sightseeing, there are two pools you can cool off in, or head to the spa for a massage with handcrafted aromatic oils.

At the all-day dining restaurant, the Cambodian chef's menu gives international dishes a Khmer twist and puts a gourmet spin on local dishes, using as much organic and locally grown produce as possible. And don't miss a sundowner at the Sky Bar.

ON YOUR DOORSTEP
A 15-minute drive from the hotel, Phare Ponleu Selpak (pharecircus.org) is not your average circus. The energetic young performers use dance, acrobatics and theatre to tell singularly Cambodian stories to sell-out crowds. Behind the scenes, the circus supports an arts school in Battambang.

$ *Doubles from US$265*

|●| *Local and international dishes with a Khmer twist*

☛ *River Rd, Siem Reap; www. jayahouseriverpark siemreap.com*

Orphanage tourism in Cambodia

Orphanage tourism is still big business in Cambodia, despite numerous studies indicating short-term visits can cause harm to a child's development and emotional wellbeing. If you'd like to help local kids, consider making a donation to the ChildSafe Movement (thinkchildsafe.org), a Cambodian-based NGO dedicated to protecting vulnerable children.

CANADA
Skwachàys Lodge

● *Participate in indigenous cultural experiences that support Aboriginal artists and performers* ● *Experience a traditional sweat lodge in the rooftop garden*

'Sustainability has always been a focus of First Nations culture,' says Maggie Edwards, general manager of Canada's first indigenous arts and culture hotel, which takes sustainability into the social environment. Not only did First Nations artists create distinctive artworks in each of the 18 guest rooms, but the boutique hotel also uses a portion of its profits to subsidize 24 housing units for indigenous artists in the same restored Victorian building. Skwachàys also offers regular cultural experiences, from indigenous art activities to spoken word events, open to guests and to the local community. Guests can also arrange traditional-style sweat lodge or smudging ceremonies with an Elder.

With a comprehensive recycling programme and eco-friendly cleaning products, environmental sustainability is taken seriously; bath amenities, coffee and other supplies are also sourced from indigenous-owned companies.

ON YOUR DOORSTEP
The art gallery on the hotel's lobby level stocks works by indigenous artists from around the region: small souvenirs, jewellery and bags, museum-quality carvings, prints, textiles, and other works. Gallery proceeds help support the hotel's housing initiatives.

$ *Doubles from CAD$179*

🍽 *Breakfast includes indigenous breads*

🐦 **29/31 W Pender St, Vancouver, BC; www.skwachays. com. The hotel is a 10-minute walk from Waterfront Station**

● **Eco-luxury** ● **Sustainable Dining**

CHILE
Winebox Valparaiso

● *Sleep in the city's first urban winery built with upcycled materials* ● *Cosy up in a chic room decorated with murals by local artists* ● *Quaff zero-kilometre wine made on-site*

Twenty-five decommissioned shipping containers from the harbour below were stacked on top of each other like a game of Tetris to create this colourful hilltop hotel in the salt-worn seaport of Valparaiso. Central Chile's second city (after the capital Santiago) is known as much for its shipping prowess as its hill-clinging communities, all of which are blanketed in world-renowned street art. That's why WineBox, too, is covered in prismatic murals from the city's top talent. Nearly everything within the hotel is made from upcycled materials, from chairs crafted out of disused sinks to benches built from bathtubs. Oh, and the wine

part? Owner Grant Phelps cut his teeth in the vineyards of the nearby Casablanca Valley and now stomps his grapes in the basement here, making it Valparaiso's first urban winery.

ON YOUR DOORSTEP
Take a walk over to Cerro Carcel to visit the Parque Cultural de Valparaiso, a vibrant cultural centre with a theatre and gallery spaces that was built to transform a site of reclusion (a dictatorship-era prison) into one of inclusion.

$ *Doubles CLP53000*

🍽 *BYO cheese to the on-site wine tastings*

🐦 **Baquedano 763, Valparaiso; www. wineboxvalparaiso. com**

CHINA (HONG KONG)

HOTEL ICON

● *Slumber at the home of Asia's largest vertical garden* ● *Chow down on a plant-based 'impossible burger' that generates 87% less emissions than a traditional burger*

Stepping into the tranquil oasis of Hotel Icon, the 8603-plant vertical garden hovering above the lobby provides the first hint that this is not your average Hong Kong accommodation. The city's first hotel to introduce an electric shuttle and implement technology that turns food waste from its three restaurants into water, it's not only a pioneer of Hong Kong sustainability, but a model for business hotels of the future.

Eco-friendly initiatives – which also include energy efficient heating, cooling and lighting systems – aside, Hotel Icon nails the guest experience with its state-of-the-art health club, open-air pool (with a plastic straw-less bar) overlooking Victoria Harbour, and luxe Angsana Spa by Banyan Tree. There's also a slick club lounge on the 28th floor that'll tempt you to upgrade to a club room.

Commanding equally impressive views over Kowloon and the harbour, the hotel's 262 business-chic rooms (which have minibars stocked with complimentary drinks and snacks) are softened with wood tones. Consistent with the hotel's eco-friendly theme, filtered water is provided as an alternative to plastic bottles, with bathroom amenities (by botanical-extract-based Australian brand Appelles) now available in reusable dispensers. Repeat guests will also notice the hotel switched from plastic to cotton laundry bags in 2019.

$ *Doubles from HK$1320*

⫶⊙⫶ *Cafe fare, Cantonese fine-dining, and a market-style buffet*

☞ 17 Science Museum Rd, Tsim Sha Tsui East, Kowloon; www. hotel-icon.com. The hotel is 7 minutes' walk from the Hung Hom international train station

Saving an estimated 40 trees per year, the paperless check-in seals the eco-friendly deal.

ON YOUR DOORSTEP
Hotel Icon lies two blocks south of the extraordinary Hong Kong Museum of History, with highlights of the 'Hong Kong Story' including a recreation of an entire arcaded street in Central from 1881 and a full-sized fishing junk.

CHINA

URBN BOUTIQUE SHANGHAI

● *Check into Shanghai's first carbon-neutral hotel* ● *Dine on delicious seafood without having to fret about its provenance* ● *Get back to nature in smart rooms furnished with recycled wood*

URBN Boutique Shanghai isn't shy about trumpeting its status as China's first carbon-neutral hotel. In a city not well known for its environmentally friendly practices, the URBN set a new standard upon its 2008 opening: in the years since, more than a dozen other sustainable-minded boutique hotels have opened across the city. Standing in the bamboo-forested lobby and admiring URBN's modern, minimalist style, you can be forgiven for not noticing that the 26-room hotel (formerly an abandoned warehouse) was built entirely with recycled construction waste. Add to that a state-of-the-art water-cooled air-con system, a seafood bistro focused on sustainably and locally sourced organic produce, and a busy cocktail lounge; and Felix Wang, the pioneering Chinese hotelier who studied sustainability abroad and dreamed of bringing it home, is right to be proud.

ON YOUR DOORSTEP
Organic produce and sustainable shopping options are increasingly in vogue in Shanghai. Organic Kitchen (organickitchenshanghai. com) was the city's first organic food delivery service, and now also has a restaurant about 15 minutes south of the hotel by taxi.

$ *Doubles CNY1200*

|◉| *Sustainable seafood*

☞ **183 Jiaozhou Rd, Jing'an District, Shanghai; www. cachethotels. com. The hotel is a 10-minute walk from Jing'an Temple metro**

WHERE DOES YOUR SEAFOOD COME FROM?

Choosing sustainable seafood has never been so important. Remove the guesswork by downloading a sustainable seafood app for your destination. The Sustainable Seafood Guide app is a great resource in Australia, while the WWF-HK Seafood Guide app is your go-to for Hong Kong. Conveniently, most sustainable seafood apps are free.

COLOMBIA

BIOHOTEL ORGANIC SUITES

● *Experience Bogotá's greenest luxury hotel* ● *Relax in the spa or help power the hotel by using its gym equipment* ● *Dine on fresh fusion food spiced with herbs from the hotel's organic garden*

Set within the leafy northern Bogotá neighbourhood of Usaquen, Biohotel Organic Suites proves just how sexy it is to be green. Designed to combine luxury, comfort and relaxation with the utmost respect for the environment, this chic urban retreat was built with water-saving systems such as an exterior green wall to collect rainwater, which mitigates greenhouse effects by improving thermal insulation of the building, and has 72 solar panels on its roof to provide most of the hotel's electricity needs. Inside, each smart, earthy-toned room – including plush junior suites with Jacuzzis – is equipped with organic linens and cotton mattresses, renewable wood furnishings, and carpets made from fully recycled materials. You can even actively participate in minimising the hotel's carbon footprint simply by hitting the gym, with the equipment designed to generate power while in use.

As for the relaxation part, there's a spa complete with a sauna and a solarium and an aquatic centre with a heated pool. You can also sign up for a bio-hydrotherapy treatment at the massage centre. And for meals, the hotel's restaurant, Green Piece, crafts its healthy dishes from meat, fish, and poultry sourced from organic suppliers, and vegetables and spices grown in the its own organic garden, with vegetarian, vegan, and gluten-free menus also available. On the

$ *Doubles from US$60*

1●1 *Organic Latin American fusion*

☛ *Carrera 7, Bis 124-36, Bogotá; www. biohotelcolombia. com*

rooftop, don't miss the photo-worthy vertical garden dripping with fresh produce and herbs.

ON YOUR DOORSTEP
For souvenirs, check out Taller de Te tea shop in Chapinero Alto, which has over 90 botanical blends made from ancestral herbs. Just a few blocks south, don't miss a meal at Salvo Patria, a restaurant that celebrates the diversity of native Colombian ingredients.

● Eco-luxury ● Sustainable Dining

CZECH REPUBLIC
Mosaic House

● Soak up Mitteleuropean style in the Czech Republic's coolest eco hotel ● Start the day with fresh, organic and homemade breakfast goodies at the on-site restaurant

Spangled with quirky design details, including a gorgeous 1930s mosaic in the lobby, this upscale hotel-and-hostel has also pulled together a mosaic of resource-saving initiatives, from greywater recycling to solar. Not only is it Prague's first carbon-neutral hotel, but it's also the first hotel in the Czech Republic to be run on 100% renewable energy sources. Wedged between the green expanse of Charles Square and the Vltava river, in the western part of Nové Město (New Town), this multilevel, style-forward place doesn't discriminate against hostel guests, offering the same clean, modular design in shared dorms as in top-floor private rooms with city views. The nearby streets, lined with 19th- and 20th-century buildings, hold museums, cafes and bars (if you make it past restobar La Loca on the ground floor).

ON YOUR DOORSTEP
If you're staying on a Saturday, make time to wander down to the river embankment at midday to enjoy the Náplavka Farmers Market. Stretching from Trojická to Výton, it sells a fantastic array of seasonal produce, baked goods, booze, charcuterie and crafts.

$ *Dorms from CZK370, doubles from CZK2400*

🍽 *Med-style fusion*

☞ **Odborů 4, Nové Město, Prague; mosaichouse.com. The hotel is a 450m walk from Karlovo náměstí metro station**

DENMARK

HOTEL OTTILIA

● *Lap up state-of-the-art tech and design features, including art installations and a snazzy app to use as your room key* ● *Tuck into a 90-100% organic breakfast*

Given its reputation as a city of bicycles, it should perhaps come as no surprise that Copenhagen has announced its aim to become the world's first carbon-neutral capital by 2025. There are more than five bikes for every car here, and tourists can use the city's simple electric bike-sharing scheme to tour spread-out attractions including its harbours, Little Mermaid statue, Christiania commune and old military fortress.

Dozens of local hotels have taken up the baton of sustainability, but none more so than those run by progressive Copenhagen hotel group Brøchner. It was the first company in Denmark to open a chemical-free hotel (the five-star Hotel Herman K), which is possible thanks to an odourless coating that makes surfaces self-disinfecting, eradicating the need for chemical-based cleaning products. Hotel Ottilia, its newest pad, opened in 2019 and has the same technology. Other sustainability features include automatic temperature controls in rooms, and air-con that reuses cold water from the local canals and harbours to cool the rooms.

Hotel Ottilia itself is an astounding work of regeneration, housed inside the old Carlsberg Brewery. Common areas have all the hallmarks of minimalist Danish design, combined with the high ceilings and industrial framework you'd expect from a manufacturing plant, while raw concrete walls give the chic rooms a tough edge. A rooftop bar-restaurant and a daily (free!) wine hour are the icing on the cake.

ON YOUR DOORSTEP

The entire neighbourhood around Hotel Ottilia is a reimagining of the old Carlsberg brewing premises, now called the Carlsberg City District. Old industrial buildings have been converted into shops, cafes and bars, punctuated by historic gardens.

$ *Doubles from DKK1250*

....

¶⦿| *Organic European rooftop dining*

....

☛ Bryggernes Plads 7, Carlsberg Byen, Copenhagen; www.brochner-hotels.com. The hotel is a 10-minute walk from Enghave Plads metro station, which is one stop from Copenhagen Central Station

FRANCE

HOTEL GAVARNI

● *Gaze toward the Eiffel Tower from your room at one of Paris' most forward-thinking hotels* ● *Fuel up at the breakfast buffet stocked entirely with organic produce*

Showing it's possible to have an eco-conscience in the poshest suburbs of Paris, Hotel Gavarni was the first independent hotel in the French capital to receive the European Ecolabel. But rather than sit back on its certification, the characterful 25-room midrange hotel encourages guests to get in on the green action by using the recycling bins provided in rooms, supporting organic producers by eating breakfast in-house, and taxi-pooling to limit sightseeing emissions (look for the sign in reception for pre-booked taxi departure times and destinations). It even covers the cost of public transport and Vélib (the city's bike-share system) for staff, and runs a blog (greenhotelsparis.com) focusing on eco-friendly city happenings. Oh yeah, and it's just across the Seine from the Eiffel Tower.

ON YOUR DOORSTEP

Need a break from cured meats and cheese? If you find yourself in Le Marais, pop into Café Pinson (cafepinson.fr) for some gluten-free, vegetarian-centric goodness; it's among a growing number of vegetarian and vegan cafes sprouting in the city.

$ *Doubles from €160*

⦿ *Organic and fair-trade French breakfast*

☛ 5 rue Gavarni, 16e, Paris; www. gavarni.com. Hotel Gavarni is less than 300m walk northwest of Passy station (metro line 6)

GERMANY
ALMODÓVAR HOTEL

● *Savour organic, vegan and vegetarian delights* ● *Recline in sustainably sourced, Bauhaus-style furniture* ● *Kick back in the rooftop sauna with views over Berlin*

The Almodóvar is Berlin's first leading hotel with sustainability at its heart. Constructed using responsibly sourced, natural components, fit together in open, pleasing designs, and pledged to an extensive list of environmentally responsible operational practices, it effortlessly demonstrates the virtues of marrying ethics with aesthetics. That's as true of the Bauhaus-style furniture crafted from sustainably managed forest wood as it is of the quality of textiles woven from organic materials. Located in the artsy Friedrichshain neighbourhood, The Almodóvar is particularly well known for Bardot's Bio Deli, its in-house restaurant where attention is lavished on vegan and vegetarian cooking using fresh, seasonal and as-local-as-possible ingredients and complemented by wines and cocktails from certified organic sources. Rounding out its offering is a dedicated rooftop wellness and spa area.

ON YOUR DOORSTEP
A 20-minute walk west of the hotel is Veganz (veganz.de), Berlin's all-vegan grocery store, with more than 160 plant-based products. Much closer, only five minutes door to door, is Lück's (luecks-berlin.de), a small restaurant committed to pure, seasonal, plant-based cuisine.

$ *Doubles from €104*

🍽 *Med-inspired vegetarian and vegan*

☞ **Boxhagener Straße 83, Berlin; www. almodovarhotel.de. The Almodóvar is a 10-minute stroll north of Ostkreuz metro station**

GUATEMALA

GOOD HOTEL ANTIGUA

● *Bed down in a colonial mansion-turned-modern boutique hotel with a small footprint and a big social conscience* ● *Learn Spanish at a local school that supports impoverished kids*

In the heart of postcard-perfect Antigua – where antiquity blends seamlessly with cosmopolitan restaurants and boutiques selling Central America's finest crafts – a colonial-era mansion has been transformed into a contemporary hotel with a cause. Divided into four room types, some with lofty mezzanines others with private patios, each of the 20 options are bright and minimalist, decked out in blonde wood and white walls, with design-forward details. The rooms mix up natural, durable and repurposed materials with local touches – a contemporary take on traditional sinks, handcrafted tiles – all made by Guatemalan artisans. In fact, everything about the hotel is local, from the organic toiletries to the handwoven blankets, the first-class coffee to the friendly staff.
Built around a green central patio, the hotel, the living room and the kitchen were designed to flow into each other, with plenty of airy communal spaces, perfect for relaxing and mingling after a day's sightseeing.
Saúl L'Osteria Antigua, the adjoining open-sided restaurant, was created with multiple spaces – convivial communal tables, cosy corners and laid-back lounging areas – and serves up authentic Neapolitan pizza, as well as hosting art exhibitions and live music.
The clincher? Good Hotel (a Dutch initiative that is going global) also supports Niños de Guatemala, an NGO that offers more than 500 underprivileged children access to education in two primary schools and a secondary school, as well as providing beyond-school training through the Good Academy programme.

ON YOUR DOORSTEP
Shop for one-of-a-kind *huipiles* (women's embroidered tunics), bags, scarves and handicrafts at the cavernous Nim Pot, a 15-minute walk northwest. As well as offering local artisans a place to sell their wares at a fair price, it helps to preserve age-old skills.

$ *Doubles from US$70*

|⦿| *Mediterranean-inspired dishes, pasta and top-notch pizza*

☛ *Calle del Hermano Pedro 12, Antigua; www. goodhotelantigua. com. Good Hotel is a 20-minute walk from Antigua's bus terminal*

HUNGARY
CASATI

● *Bed down in an adults-only bower of art and sophistication, where the indulgence comes with green credentials* ● *Relax in the on-site sauna after a day exploring Budapest*

Adaptive reuse, one of the most sensible and aesthetically pleasing strategies for sustainability, is brilliantly demonstrated in this charismatic 25-room boutique hotel, occupying an 18th-century Budapest building wrapped around an unusual covered courtyard. And sustainability is clearly in this hotel's DNA: measures such as recycled-only paper, LED lighting throughout, eco-friendly cleaning and strict energy- and waste-measurement have earned Casati recognition within Hungary for its green credentials. And the care they've expended on generating an air of sophistication, splattering eclectic artworks about the walls and concocting individual decorative schemes for its themed rooms, is reflected in the no-children (14+ only) policy. Despite not housing a restaurant, it's an inviting place to linger, with a wonderfully quirky, Shanghai-inspired, cocktail-slinging gay bar, Tuk Tuk, on the ground floor; try an 'Asian Pornstar'.

ON YOUR DOORSTEP
Sophistication doesn't stop at the door with Casati: cultural diversions abound in this sector of Budapest, from the Budapesti Operettszínház (Vaudeville Theatre) to the Madách Színház (Theatre) and the Magyar Állami Operaház (Hungarian State Opera).

$ *Doubles from €96*

🍽 *Buffet breakfast featuring local produce*

☛ **Paulay Ede utca 31, Budapest; www.casatibudapesthotel.com. The hotel is just a minute's walk from Opera metro station**

ICELAND
EYJA GULDSMEDEN

● *Lounge in Scandi-chic rooms designed with natural materials* ● *Fuel up on organic breakfasts with homemade skyr, Icelandic salmon, kleinur (local doughnuts) and hafragrautur (warm oatmeal)*

The dramatic natural blueprint of blistering volcanic crust and powerful waters that secured Iceland's tourism potential has also helped it become a world leader in renewable energy. Geothermal and hydropower account for the country's electricity, and Reykjavik aims to completely ditch fossil fuels by 2050.

In the heart of downtown Reykjavik, Eyja Guldsmeden makes a fitting base for low-impact exploration. Housed in a former office block, the hotel's interior is a trademark of the Guldsmeden chain: minimalist Scandinavian style mixed with natural tones and textures. Guldsmeden is a Danish company, but Eyja is locally owned. Sustainable, organic and local products are key to the guest experience at Eyja, Iceland's first hotel to be awarded Green Globe certification, which means bamboo toothbrushes, paper cups, eco-certified bath products and no single-use plastic.

ON YOUR DOORSTEP
Iceland's lava fields, steamy natural pools and snow-capped mountains unfold just beyond Reykjavic's boundaries, but the city itself is packed with Viking history, cutting-edge design and an exciting contemporary dining scene. Don't miss the National Museum, Settlement Exhibition and zany Hallgrímskirkja church.

$ *Doubles from €160*

🍽 *Local and organic, with vegan options*

☛ **Brautarholt 10-14, Reykjavik; www.hoteleyja.is**

IRELAND
Iveagh Gardens Hotel

● Tip your hat to Ireland's most ambitious sustainable hotel ● Discover a rare hotel bistro that caters to vegans ● Sip craft cocktails with house-made syrups

Named for the gorgeous adjoining Iveagh Gardens, a set of green 'lungs' landscaped in the 19th century, this four-star stunner aspires to create the smallest carbon footprint of any comparable hotel in Europe. Its means are ingenious: harnessing energy from an aquifer to drive the heating and cooling; an on-site gas turbine minimising reliance on the grid; gravity-fed wastewater systems; smart-controlled LED lighting; and low-energy lifts. Whether staying in a smaller, funkier 'city pod', or a grand, balconied suite overlooking the gardens, it's good to know an indulgent weekend spent here among pretty Georgian and Victorian streets isn't emitting carbon into the atmosphere. Elle's, the on-site bar and restaurant, looks after vegans as happily as it does the cocktail set, with delicious plant-powered dining options for every course of the main menu.

ON YOUR DOORSTEP
Many of Dublin's biggest draws are within easy walking distance of the Iveagh Garden: Trinity College; the National Museum, National Gallery and Little Museum of Ireland; Dublin Castle; St Stephen's Green; and the clamour and culture of Grafton St.

$ *Doubles from €98*

⦿l *Euro-bistro fare*

☛ **72/74 Harcourt St, St Kevin's, Dublin; www. iveaghgardenhotel.ie**

ISRAEL

Fauzi Azar Inn

● *Meet members of the Old City community on guided walks* ● *Learn spoken Arabic and traditional Nazarene recipes in classes taught by locals*

Two centuries ago, the wealthy Azar family built a grand mansion in the heart of Nazareth, site of the Annunciation and childhood home of Jesus Christ. Today, their grand Ottoman home welcomes travellers as part of a collaborative effort between kibbutz-raised Maoz Inon, visionary founder of the Abraham Hostels and Suraida Shomar Nasser, Nazareth-born granddaughter of the family patriarch, the late Fauzi Azar. Conceived as a meeting place for people of all cultures, nationalities and faiths, Fauzi Azar Inn has been a driving force behind the revitalisation of the old city, encouraging local families to open guesthouses, shops and restaurants with the goal of creating a dynamic, sustainable tourist ecosystem in the long-neglected centre of Nazareth, Israel's largest Arab city.

An oasis of calm steeped in Nazarene and Palestinian history, the guesthouse has 14 rooms offering both dorm beds and private accommodation. But Fauzi Azar's most glorious architecture is to be found in its public spaces. The plant-filled open courtyard, accented by Ottoman-style stone arches, is great for chilling out and meeting fellow travellers, as is the lounge, whose soaring ceilings were hand-painted in the 1860s. On offer are Arabic lessons, cooking classes and free walking tours that introduce visitors to local history, culture

and shop owners. Fauzi Azar's staff split their time between helping run the guesthouse and contributing to the local community in various ways, such as teaching English.

ON YOUR DOORSTEP
Fauzi Azar Inn is a short walk from Nazareth's most important churches and the start of the Jesus Trail (jesustrail.com), a 65km walking path linking Nazareth with Capernaum, on the shores of the Sea of Galilee.

$ *Dorm beds from US$25, doubles from US$125*

🍽 *Try local delicacies at Nazareth's souk just a few streets away*

☛ *6112 St, No 9, Old City, Nazareth; www. abrahamhostels.com/ nazareth. Nazareth lies 100km north of the capital Tel Aviv. Buses from Tel Aviv stop 1.5km from the inn on the city's ring road*

IDENTIFYING A SUSTAINABLE SLEEP

Gone are the days when a vague commitment to conserving water and electricity was the marker of an eco-friendly hotel. Today, a growing number of accommodations have implemented innovative strategies to become more environmentally and socially sustainable. The rise of greenwashing, however, can make it difficult to separate hotels striving for best practices from those simply pretending to. Here are four key signs your hotel is committed to the cause.

IT HAS A SUSTAINABILITY POLICY

A hotel committed to sustainability will almost always have a sustainability policy on its website. This will spell out if it has been certified by a credible organisation such as EarthCheck or Leadership in Energy and Environmental Design (LEED) and flag specific sustainability initiatives it has implemented. If you can't find this information online, contact the hotel. If they can't provide specifics, be wary. Keep in mind that smaller hotels often struggle to afford the oft-expensive improvements required to meet certification criteria, so don't be too quick to judge accommodation providers on that basis alone.

IT'S COMMITTED TO LIMITING ITS ENVIRONMENTAL IMPACT

Hotels that have had sustainability at heart from conception are generally more low-impact, but many other hotels have done a commendable job of greening up their act. Beyond the implementation of energy and water-conserving technologies, initiatives to look out for include an on-site garden that supplies the hotel restaurant, rooftop beehives, single-use plastic-free amenities, locally made furnishings, recycling bins in guest rooms, the use of eco-friendly cleaning products, and washing linens only on request.

IT WORKS CLOSELY WITH THE LOCAL COMMUNITY

Sustainable hotels empower local communities. This typically takes the form of hiring local staff (and providing adequate training and paying them fairly), using local suppliers, supporting sustainable community programmes, and integrating guests with the community on the community's terms, such as via tours run by locals that support local businesses and encourage the preservation of cultural traditions.

IT ENCOURAGES GUESTS TO GET INVOLVED

A truly sustainable hotel will inspire guests to follow their lead by incorporating interactive initiatives, such as offering reusable water bottles and/or filtered water refills, free or cheap bicycle rental or shared transport options, guest experiences that support local people and businesses, incentives for guests who arrive by public transport or opt out of having their room serviced, and hosting environmental clean-up events. Sustainable hotels also typically encourage guests verbally to support the hotel's mission upon check-in.

Right: Winebox Valparaiso, Chile (p172)

● Eco-luxury ● Sustainable Dining

ITALY
HOTEL MILANO SCALA

● *Sip organic wine at the leafy rooftop bar* ● *Sample novel vegan and vegetarian restaurant fare* ● *Slumber in luxe rooms with emission-free heating and air-con*

What's on display at Hotel Milano Scala, Milan's first zero-emissions hotel, is as gratifying as what's unseen. From the outside, it's a tasteful luxury hotel committed to musical culture and set in an ornate, historical, 19th-century palazzo. Inside, however, is a deeply felt and comprehensively practised devotion to sustainable hospitality. During a €13-million interior renovation completed in 2010, the hotel was fitted with a state-of-the-art system that measures and tracks everything from energy consumption to temperature control, the latter managed by tapping naturally hot water from Milan's aquifer. Other touches include an organic roof garden, a green and local ('glocal') restaurant and even an electric company car. It's sophisticated proof that a modern, urban, boutique hotel can have a green body and soul.

ON YOUR DOORSTEP
Facing the hotel is an L'Erbolario (erbolario. com) store selling sustainably produced plant-based cosmetics. A 15-minute metro ride away, innovative eco-conscious bar and restaurant Gesto (gestofailtuo.it) is a great spot for cocktails and creative small plates with ethically sourced produce.

$ *Doubles from €230*

🍴 *Organic, seasonal Italian cuisine*

☛ **Via dell'Orso 7, Milan; www. hotelmilanoscala.it. The hotel is in the central Brera district, handy for tram lines 1 and 2, and metro lines 1 and 3**

● Eco-luxury ● Community Interaction

KENYA
WILDEBEEST ECO CAMP

● *Sleep off your jet-lag in a rustic-chic glamping tent in an urban oasis* ● *Meet locals while exploring one of Nairobi's safer neighbourhoods*

A haven in hectic Nairobi, Wildebeest cushions city stays with its tropical garden, infinity pool, firepit and decks for easing into Kenya with a cup of local coffee. More than just a handy-for-the-airport hotel, it supports local community projects, including a day care centre, an orphanage and a youth centre (though child welfare experts recommend against visiting these).

The lodge's eco-initiatives are numerous, from solar lighting and water harvesting to employing staff from marginalised tribes and planting native plants that encourage butterflies. There are grassy campsites, dorms and safari tents, including the solar-powered en-suite deluxe tent, as well as cottage rooms for guests seeking four walls after a long expedition. Wildebeest is deservedly a staple of eco-conscious backpackers' itineraries, while facilities such as the kids' playground and travel desk cater to families and Kenya newbies.

ON YOUR DOORSTEP
Wildebeest is close to Nairobi National Park and the Giraffe Centre. Also nearby are the Karen Blixen Museum, the *Out of Africa* author's former home, and the David Sheldrick Wildlife Trust's Orphans' Projects, which featured in the BBC series *Elephant Diaries*.

$ *Doubles US$106*

🍴 *Light lunches, buffet dinners*

☛ **Mokoyeti Rd W, Langata, Nairobi; www.wildebeest ecocamp.com**

MEXICO

HOTEL CON CORAZÓN OAXACA

● *Learn the secret to cooking Oaxacan cuisine at a stylish eco-sensitive hotel*
● *Visit craft villages with a local guide* ● *Meet local interns that the hotel sponsors*

Part hotel, part social enterprise, Hotel con Corazón is genuinely a hotel with heart. Designed by a Portuguese, Oaxaca-based architect, it nods to the city's Spanish colonial style but it's lighter and brighter, with lots of glass and open terraces and patios.

The 14 rooms have high-ends beds and showers but are simply decorated with lots of Oaxacan details. And like the first Hotel Con Corazón in Granada, Nicaragua, almost everything is custom-made locally to help support the city's artisans: handloomed textiles, handcrafted furniture, hand-thrown pottery. And the lamps are made from jicara, a local fruit.

Oaxaca is one of the most beautiful cities in Mexico but the state is one the country's poorest, with limited employment opportunities, so the hotel invests 100% of its profits into local education. It also sponsors school scholarships for 10 students, as well as internships with a local high school and work experience for young people, so you'll meet those you're helping to support.

Just a 15-minute walk to the Zócalo, Oaxaca's historic heart, it makes the perfect base to explore the city's colonial splendour, indigenous traditions and world-class cuisine. The hotel can help arrange tours to archaeological sites, sleepy villages with vibrant crafts, and hiking in the Sierra Madre. It can also organise in-house

$ *Doubles from US$86*

🍽 *Hearty Oaxacan breakfast with top-notch local coffee*

☛ **Calle División Oriente 129, Oaxaca City; www.hotelconcorazon.com. It's a 15-minute taxi ride from Oaxaca's international airport and a 10-minute drive from the ADO bus terminal**

cooking classes and you'll get a real taste of rural life visiting a *palenque* (distillery) to discover what goes in to the fiery local spirit, mezcal.

ON YOUR DOORSTEP
Set up by female artisans in 1992, Mujeres Artesanias de las Regiones de Oaxaca was one of the city's first cooperative-run stores – now around 80 women sell their handwoven textiles there. It's located at 5 Cinco de Mayo 204, 15 minutes' walk east of the hotel.

MEXICO

THE LOCAL WAY

● *Support Mexican entrepreneurship and craftwork by bedding down in a local-owned apartment* ● *Feel like you live in Mexico City's most vibrant neighbourhoods*

As Mexico City's premier locally owned apartment rental company, The Local Way offers accommodation in the best areas of the cosmopolitan capital. Though no two properties are the same, sustainability is a common thread, from artworks and furnishings produced almost entirely by local Mexican craftspeople to eco-friendly features like biodegradable cleaning products, eco-filters for drinking water and recycling bins that come with instructions.

The luxurious apartments are dotted throughout a number of neighbourhoods, from Polanco, a ritzy borough just north of Bosque de Chapultepec – the largest green area of the city – full of colonial-style mansions, embassies, restaurants and luxury stores, to Roma, an eclectic cultural hub for gastronomy, nightlife, and contemporary art galleries. Accommodation ranges from one-bedroom apartments to three-bedroom suites ideal for families, each featuring living rooms, dining areas, and fully equipped kitchens; some even come with extensive private outdoor spaces and communal areas, such as gyms, outdoor pools, and spas. You'll enjoy the convenience of top-level service you would expect at the city's finest hotels, with the added privacy of feeling like you're in your own home – plus, an on-call concierge is available 24-hours through WhatsApp to make dinner reservations and even book personalised tours that support fellow Mexican-owned businesses.

ON YOUR DOORSTEP

Each accommodation is located near a park, from Roma suites set within easy range of convivial Río de Janeiro Square to Condesa homes located only a five-minute walk to Parque México and Parque España, two of Mexico City's main green spaces.

$ *Doubles from US$120*

🍽 *Apartments are stocked with Mexican snacks and craft beer*

☛ *Various* **neighbourhoods, Mexico City; www. thelocalwaymx.com. The Local Way can arrange private pick-up from Mexico City International Airport, or you can take the metro**

MONACO
HOTEL METROPOLE

● *Stay in a historic luxury hotel that's moving with the times* ● *Work your way through the vegetarian menu designed by the late Michelin-starred chef Joël Robuchon*

Best known for its glamour and excess, Monaco might not be the first destination that springs to mind when it comes to sustainability. But the city-state's only independently owned luxury hotel has been working hard to change that narrative. Priding itself on being 'a respectful luxury destination', the Hotel Metropole's 'Green Attitude' policy might be discreet to discerning luxury travellers, but initiatives implemented by its Green Committee over the past decade make it significant.

With two Michelin-starred restaurants, a Givenchy spa (one of only three worldwide), and a rooftop pool designed by the late Karl Lagerfeld, the Belle Époque hotel offers a classic Mediterranean luxury experience. Behind the scenes, it's working to continuously reduce its energy and water consumption, and is involved in various humanitarian and environmental causes. All staff members are trained up on the Metrople's environmental strategy, and preference is given to suppliers that share the hotel's goals.

Guests will also notice that Hotel Metropole has switched plastic straws for a biodegradable alternative (the first hotel in Monaco to do so), with plastic bottles banned in 2019. Electric cars are available for transportation, and after checking in, you'll find an informative in-room request to 'act green' during your stay.

$ *Doubles from €357*

....

🍽 *Haute Mediterranean and Japanese cuisine featuring seasonal local produce*

....

☛ **4 avenue de la Madone, Monte Carlo; www. metropole.com. Trains run between Nice and Gare de Monaco, just 1km west of the Metropole**

Committed to serving seasonal local produce and sustainable seafood, the hotel's four restaurants – with menus created by the late 'chef of the century' Joël Robuchon – also demonstrate that luxury experiences don't need to come at the expense of the planet.

ON YOUR DOORSTEP
It's only 4 minutes' walk to the Casino Monte Carlo, but guests can also opt to tour the nearby Terre de Monaco – one of the world's largest private organic urban farms – with hotel chef Christophe Cussac, who will prepare a meal with your harvest.

NEPAL

DWARIKA'S HOTEL

● Sleep in a museum-like hotel that celebrates the city's architectural heritage ● Take a sustainable culinary journey of Nepal at the organic farm-supplied degustation restaurant

 Described as a 'living museum', this family-run luxury hotel near Kathmandu's airport has become a saviour for Newari architecture, dating back to the Malla dynasty (1201–1769). In the 1970s, Indian-born founder Dwarika Das Shrestha built his namesake hotel in the red-brick style of the Kathmandu valley's palaces, incorporating into the design Newari wooden carvings salvaged from the streets of Kathmandu and beyond as the city began its march towards modernisation in the 1950s.

Continually expanded over the years, the 83-room property, which wraps around a lush central courtyard with one of the city's only swimming pools, has evolved into the ultimate showpiece of indigenous design.

To help preserve the art of Newari carving that makes it so unique, an on-site wood workshop teaches young craftspeople the ancient skill, now particularly valuable as the city continues to rebuild its Newari temples damaged in the 2015 earthquake.

On top of its commitment to cultural preservation (the Dwarika's offers daily free yoga classes), the hotel has also taken measures to reduce its environmental footprint by minimising single-use plastics from its bathrooms, and sources produce for its three on-site restaurants (as well as charming Kaiser Cafe in Thamel) from its own organic farms. The more complex task of implementing a sustainable alternative to the single-use water bottles supplied in the antique-packed guestrooms is in the hotel's longer-term plans.

ON YOUR DOORSTEP
The Dwarika's is handy for two top city sights: Shree Pashupatinath Temple with its Hindu funeral ghats (15 minutes' walk), and Boudhanath, Nepal's largest Buddhist stupa (15 minutes' drive). Taxis line up in front of the hotel.

$ *Doubles from US$265*

🍽 *Nepali and Japanese fine dining and international bistro fare*

☛ **Battisputali Rd, Kathmandu; www. dwarikas.com**

AVOIDING PLASTIC WATER BOTTLES IN NEPAL

Relying on bottled water might seem like a necessity in countries lacking clean tap water, but if you forget to pack a water purifying device for your next trip to Nepal, there's a simple way to avoid this. Aquatabs water purifying tablets are available very cheaply in Nepal's ubiquitous pharmacies. Unlike iodine tablets of the past, Aquatabs barely have any taste, so there's no need for a flavouring agent.

● Eco-luxury   ● Sustainable Dining   ● Community Interaction

NETHERLANDS
Conscious Hotel Westerpark

● *Sleep in style at the Netherlands' first wind-powered hotel* ● *Dine on 100% organic produce from local suppliers* ● *Mingle with locals at the next-door cultural hub*

With a name like Conscious Hotels, it's no surprise the Dutch boutique hotel group is all about sustainability, but the newest of its four Amsterdam properties also has bragging rights for being the first wind-powered hotel in the Netherlands. One side overlooks the buzzy Westergas arts complex, the other a tranquil green space, and it's just a 10-minute cycle from Jordaan and the city's historic centre.

Rooms are spacious, stylish and streamlined, with comfortable beds and large windows, and all materials are cradle-to-cradle, recycled or vintage. Downstairs, the all-day dining Kantoor bar and restaurant serves up creative dishes made with all-organic local ingredients – think lamb shank, Atlantic wolffish or yellow coconut curry, rounded off with vegan banana bread and cacao sorbet. Wash it down with an organic craft beer.

ON YOUR DOORSTEP
Putting the design flair into fair trade, Nukuhiva (nukuhiva.nl), a 20-minute walk southeast, is the place to go for fashion, accessories and shoes for both men and women that put people and nature first.

$ *Doubles from €75*

🍽 *Seasonal food, many veggie options*

☛ **Haarlemmerweg 10, Amsterdam; www.conscioushotels. com**

● **Sustainable Dining**   ● **Community Interaction**

NORWAY
PS:HOTELL

● *Queue alongside locals for the legendary weekday lunch buffet* ● *Meet Norwegians from all walks of life at this innovative social responsibility project*

Just a block from the Akerselva river in Oslo's vibrant Grünerløkka neighbourhood, the city's smallest hotel is also one of its most innovative. Focusing on employing people who've struggled to gain a foothold in the labour market for various reasons, PS:hotell offers guests the opportunity to support its award-winning social responsibility programme simply by booking one of its 31 simple but comfortable rooms. You can also sample some of Oslo's best coffee at the on-site Hendrix Ibsen cafe, or enjoy a meal at the hotel's restaurant specialising in homestyle meals showcasing fresh Norwegian ingredients, which offers additional opportunities for disadvantaged people to upskill.

The hotel building is part of the Vulcan sustainable urban development, which shares resources and energy. Indeed, the next-door Scandic Vulcan hotel (Norway's first energy class A hotel) collaborates on the PS:hotell's staff training programme.

ON YOUR DOORSTEP
The hotel sits opposite Mathallen (mathallenoslo. no), the city's first food hall, which features more more than 30 dining options and specialty shops specialising in high-quality products from small-scale regional producers.

$ *Doubles from NOK1670*

....

🍴 *Quality local fare*

....

☞ *Vulcan 22, Grünerløkka, Oslo; www.pshotell.no*

● Eco-luxury ● Sustainable Dining

PORTUGAL
NEYA LISBOA HOTEL

● *Sleep in sustainable style, thanks to the hotel's energy-saving and environmental policies* ● *Dine on Michelin-star quality dishes crafted from local produce*

In a quiet neighbourhood just outside the city centre, this contemporary hotel is in a rehabilitated rundown building, with added solar panels and furniture created from recycled materials. Smart rooms come with plenty of amenities, such as shiatsu massage pillows and outsized TVs, making it a hit with both business and leisure travellers. The hotel also developed an app to help guests explore Lisbon's *bairros* in the most sustainable way – on foot or using the hotel's complimentary bikes. After a hard day's sightseeing, wallow in the Jacuzzi or head to the spa for a rejuvenating massage or pampering beauty treatment with all-natural products.

As for dining, the menu at on-site restaurant Viva Lisboa was created by a Michelin star chef with a focus on Mediterranean-influenced dishes using seasonal, local produce. Don't miss the moreish *pastéis de nata* (Portuguese custard tarts) at breakfast.

ON YOUR DOORSTEP
Held monthly, Anjos70 (anjos70.org) is Lisbon's coolest alternative market, just a 10-minute walk from the hotel. Expect more than 100 stalls offering everything from vintage clothing to rare vinyl and artisan chocolates, with DJs providing the soundtrack.

$ *Doubles from €96*

|◉| *Classy cuisine*

☛ **Rua De Dona Estefânia 71-77, Lisbon; www. neyahotels.com**

RWANDA

THE RETREAT

● *Stay in Kigali's first solar-powered boutique hotel* ● *Cool off in one of two saltwater pools* ● *Savour some of Rwanda's most creative farm-to-table fare*

Kigali is emerging as an epicentre of artistry and progressive sustainability in East Africa thanks to outposts, such as The Retreat, the city's first eco-friendly, solar-powered boutique hotel. Guests adore the property, owned by US expats Alissa and Josh Ruxin, for its lavish amenities, but admire it for its function as an incubator of local talent, from elevating the work of artisans who crafted the hotel with sustainable Tanzanian teak to training a team of local chefs who run Fusion, the property's farm-to-table, all-day restaurant, offering international dishes made with local ingredients, such as cassava leaf bruschetta and sweet potato tortelli with brown butter and sage.

Replete with private patios and bathrooms with indoor-outdoor rain showers, the expansive suites are complemented by two saltwater pools, a Jacuzzi, daily yoga classes, and myriad spa treatments, including hot stone and aromatherapy massages with lotions and oils produced by organic Kenyan skincare line Cinnabar Green.

A handy base for easing into Rwanda en route to a gorilla tracking safari in Volcanoes National Park, the hotel also encourages guests to spread their tourism dollars around the capital with the help of Heaven Tours, which offers cultural experiences ranging from private basket-weaving classes with the female artisans of Nyamirambo Women's Center, to art lessons with painters and muralists, to on-site banana-wine making workshops and cooking classes.

ON YOUR DOORSTEP

The property is within a short drive of female-owned businesses, such as Question Coffee, a cafe empowering 30,000 women in rural Rwanda, and The Women's Bakery, a social enterprise teaching women how to both make and sell nutritious, affordable bread like honey tresses and banana-peanut muffins.

$ *Doubles US$600*

🍽 *International cuisine with Rwandan flavors*

☛ **5 KN29 St, Kigali; www.heavenrwanda. com/retreat.php. The Retreat is located 10km (or 20 minutes' drive) from Kigali International Airport, and is best reached by booking a private transfer directly with the property**

SINGAPORE
Parkroyal On Pickering

● *Enjoy a good night's sleep in Singapore's most cutting-edge eco-friendly slumber pad*
● *Tuck into tasty plant-based nosh at in-house Lime restaurant*

Singapore has been striving to keep things clean and green since the 1960s when then-Prime minister Lee Kuan Yew planted a *mempat* (cherry blossom) tree to signify the city-state's commitment to becoming a 'garden city'. More than five decades on, Singapore is full of fantastic green spaces. Among the best, is a hotel.

Crowned the World's Leading Green City Hotel at the 2018 World Travel Awards, Parkroyal on Pickering is architecturally designed to seamlessly blend technology with the environment, with clever design features to help decrease its environmental footprint. The open-sided concept, fluid curves and short building depth allows for maximum internal natural light, and the abundance of waterfalls and self-sustaining landscaped roof terraces and vertical gardens help to keep the building blissfully cool.

Internally, the hotel speaks to its claim of being a 'hotel-in-a-garden' with an array of greenery at every turn, while sensors monitor everything from light levels to water usage to carbon dioxide, and work together to ensure the hotel is operating efficiently around the clock.

Once ensconced in your slick, earthy-toned room, you'll find recycling bins and refillable glass water bottles. Plastic straws have been replaced with a biodegradable potato starch-derived alternative, and looking to the future, the hotel is actively exploring greener alternatives to other in-room amenities, food waste and plastic use.

ON YOUR DOORSTEP
Seek out wholesome food and enjoy eco-friendly retail therapy at nearby multi-concept store The Social Space (thesocialspace.co). Here all products come with an environmental conscience, from the nifty household products refill station to the non-toxic nail salon. The shop also actively employs marginalised people.

$ *Doubles from S$320*

....

❧❶❙ *International buffet and plant-based a la carte*

....

☞ ***3 Upper Pickering St; www.panpacific. com. The hotel is located two blocks northeast of Chinatown MRT***

SLOVENIA
Hotel Park

● *Enjoy sweet treats laced with honey from the hotel's beehives* ● *Meet locals at open events held on the hotel rooftop or in the revitalised park opposite*

Slovenia is one of the world's most sustainable countries and the unassuming Hotel Park is leading the charge in the capital Ljubljana. When the city was designated European Green Capital in 2016, the earthy-hued midrange hotel took numerous steps to reduce energy usage and waste. Reusable plastics, water-saving technology and low-energy lighting have all become core to its *modus operandi*. Virtually 100% of its waste is recycled. Tesla electric car charging stations have been installed. There's even beehives on the roof producing honey for the hotel restaurant.

Community and education are also important, as you'll glean from events such as free community yoga, library in the park and the neighbourhood litter pick-ups it gets involved with. One of the hotel's most unique features is its 'Go Green, Act Green' app, enabling guests to measure the carbon footprint of their holiday.

ON YOUR DOORSTEP
Ljubljana has more than 500 sq m of public green space per resident and a historic core that is closed to traffic: perfect for leisurely walking and cycling. Use the cheap bike-sharing scheme, Bicikelj, to explore the leafy banks of Ljubljanica River.

$ *Doubles from €80*

🍽 *Slovenian and Indian cuisine*

☛ **Tabor 9, Ljubljana; www.hotelpark. si. The hotel is a 10-minute walk from Ljubljana's main train station. Book direct and arrive by train to get a 15% discount**

SPAIN
Zalamera Bed & Breakfast

● *Enjoy a fair-trade breakfast of locally sourced cereals, juices and more*
● *Relax on the penthouse's sunny private terrace*

Modern architecture, Roman ruins, and possibly the best paella you'll find in Spain: these are just a few of the reasons to visit the colourful, beachside city of Valencia. But since 2015, there's another reason: Zalamera Bed & Breakfast. The boutique hotel is bright and airy with modern Scandinavian-meets-Spanish design; expect pops of yellow and warm woods in the rooms. But the best part of the downtown B&B is the significant commitment it's made towards sustainability, which can be difficult to find in Spain's urban hotels. They serve fair-trade and locally sourced products, such as cereal and shampoo, and heat all water for the hotel's 18 rooms with biofuel. Cabinetry is locally sourced and made by hand, and guests can explore the city on foot or by bike (€10 a day) to keep their carbon footprint low.

ON YOUR DOORSTEP
Zalamera is close to Valencia's tourist centre; you can easily bike to Jardins de Real or the historical Torres de Serranos. There are also plenty of unique restaurants nearby, including Copenhagen, a vegetarian kitchen with a three-course tasting menu for under €12.

$ *Doubles from €56*

🍽 *Fair-trade continental breakfast*

☛ **Carrer de Pelai 44, València; www. zalamerabnb.com. The hotel is a block west of València Nord train station**

THAILAND
YARD HOSTEL

● *Enjoy breakfast homemade with local ingredients* ● *Meet plugged-in locals in one of Bangkok's coolest neighbourhoods while staying at a pioneering eco-hostel*

You don't have to be a millionaire environmentalist to live a sustainable life amid the urban sprawl. Cities don't come much more urban than Bangkok, and Yard Hostel is flying the flag for a new model of environmentally friendly big city living on a small budget. Recycling is just one of many social initiatives at the hostel, to the level that even the buildings are recycled – rooms had a past life as shipping containers before being insulated with recycled paper to keep out the tropical heat.

Set in an enclosed garden, Yard enthusiastically supports the environmental cause – guests are provided with reusable water bottles to refill with purified water from a shared water station, low-energy lighting is triggered and turned off by motion sensors and timers, and the yoghurt and jam served for breakfast is handmade on the premises. And room rates help fund good causes, such as Karen community forest conservation projects.

But this still feels like a proper Thai hostel, down to the free wi-fi and yoga classes and the library of well-thumbed travel novels and guidebooks. The name is a riff on the Thai meaning of *yard* (relative) and staying here does feel like visiting an eccentric family member who is happily doing their own thing, regardless of what the neighbours say. Wrapped up in this

$ *Dorm beds from THB550*

🍽 *Thai cuisine*

☞ **51 Phahon Yothin 5, Samsen Nai, Phaya Thai, Bangkok; www.theyardhostel. com. Yard Hostel is northwest of Bangkok's historic heart, an easy 5-minute stroll from the Ari BTS Skytrain station**

urban oasis, you'll hardly notice that the edgy streets of Ari are just outside the front gate.

ON YOUR DOORSTEP
The BTS Skytrain provides a low-carbon way to explore the newer parts of Bangkok and the legendary Chatuchak Weekend Market. To reach the historic old quarter of Ratanakosin, you'll have to finish your journey on foot or by taxi.

● Eco-luxury ● Sustainable Dining

UK
QBIC HOTEL

● *Grab a tasty meal in the low-food-mile-focused Motley restaurant* ● *Book an in-room massage through a mobile spa service that uses natural aromatherapy oils*

Set in London's gritty-chic East End, Qbic has retrofitted a nondescript building with modular hotel suites playfully decorated in keeping with the character of the creative neighbourhood. Beyond the upcycled furnishings (think: garden-hose lampshades) the hotel has sustainability bedded into its core. Solar panels on the roof generate most of the hotel's power; guests are rewarded for opting out of having their room serviced with a free drink in the downstairs bar; and when your room is cleaned, it's done with 100% chemical-free products. The attached Motley restaurant's food philosophy is vegetables first and low food-miles, and you're encouraged to walk, cycle or use London's abundant public transport to reduce your carbon footprint, and save a few quid while you're at it.

ON YOUR DOORSTEP
Looking for a unique souvenir? Spend a day rummaging through the secondhand bric-a-brac, vintage wares and artworks of Brick Lane Sunday Market in Shoreditch – just a 10-minute stroll north of Qbic.

$ *Doubles from £60*

🍽 *Veggie sharing plates*

☞ *42 Adler St, Whitechapel, London; www.qbichotels. com. Qbic is close to Aldgate East and Whitechapel tube stations*

USA

1 HOTEL BROOKLYN BRIDGE

● *Soak up splendid city views from the rooftop garden* ● *Treat your taste buds to farm-to-table flavours* ● *Mingle with locals at hotel events open to the public*

The view from the rooftop garden (complete with bar and plunge pool) is hard to beat, taking in a sweeping panorama of some of NYC's greatest hits: the Statue of Liberty and New York Harbor, a skyscraper-filled Downtown Manhattan skyline and, so close it's like you can touch it, the Brooklyn Bridge. That the structure beneath you is a work of sustainable architecture and operations is almost an afterthought. But look a little closer and the LEED Gold-certified building reveals its eco-credentials. Constructed of natural and reclaimed materials like barn wood and industrial steel, it's packed with sustainable alternatives to things you may not have realised needed them: wire hangers made of recycled materials, guest keys fabricated from recycled wood, in-room upcycled chalkboards for notes. There are also native plants in green leafy abundance, while hidden from view are extensive energy, water, air and plastic-reduction programs that keep the hotel's footprint small.

Health, wellness and community are also central to the hotel's mission. A lobby cafe, ground-floor restaurant spilling into Brooklyn Bridge Park and 10th-floor cocktail lounge, open to all, feature healthy, farm-to-table cuisine. And the Bamford Haybarn Spa showcases holistic, restorative treatments and beauty products made from natural and organic ingredients. Additionally, the hotel hosts public paid-access events, such as sports fitness classes and film releases (in its private screening room) to benefit charity partners.

ON YOUR DOORSTEP

Nearby Dumbo is a bastion of ethical businesses. For food, there's Seamore's, a sustainable seafood-centric options; Luke's Lobster, a traceable sustainable lobster restaurant; and Brooklyn Roasting Company's organic and sustainable coffees.

$ *Doubles from USD$300*

|◉| *Market-driven, farm-to-table American comfort food*

☛ 60 Furman St, Brooklyn, New York; www.1hotels.com/brooklyn-bridge. The hotel is located at Pier 1 on Brooklyn Bridge Park, 250m from NYC Ferry's Dumbo terminal and a 10-minute walk from various subway lines

USA
SHORE HOTEL

● *Watch the sun set over the Santa Monica Pier from a solar-heated hot tub*
● *Relax on a private balcony just steps from the beach* ● *Laze by an energy-efficient pool*

Quintessential California unfolds in beachside Santa Monica, which has a pace of life that feels light years from LA's gridlock. The Shore Hotel is in the heart of it all, immediately across the street from the world's only solar-powered Ferris wheel, which twirls late into the night atop the Santa Monica Pier.

The LEED Gold–certified hotel doesn't leave environmental impact to chance: Everything from water reduction and energy performance to resource conservation and responsible material sourcing was built into its literal foundation. That ethos is equally present throughout the guest experience, whether lathering up with complimentary Raw Elements reef-safe sunscreen by the heated pool or Jacuzzi (both solar powered), cruising 35km of oceanfront bike path on one of the hotel's bicycles, or hydrating with plastic-free bottled water between reps at the gym, where the floor is made from recycled tyres.

ON YOUR DOORSTEP

Heal the Bay Aquarium, a non-profit that supports LA's watersheds, and the Santa Monica Farmers Market, which uses only recyclable or compostable products, are both within 800m. A short bike ride away, the Annenberg Community Beach House is the country's only public beach house.

$ *Doubles from US$349*

🍽 *Simple pool menu*

☛ *1515 Ocean Ave, Santa Monica, CA; www.shorehotel.com*

ZAMBIA

LATITUDE 15°

● *Relax post-safari in a stylish hotel filled with regional art* ● *Visit the artists behind the works that decorate your rooms* ● *Meet locals at the on-site co-working space*

Set amid southeast Lusaka's tree-lined avenues, Latitude 15° is the ultimate urban refuge for travellers in transit to or from Zambia's wildlife-rich national parks. Inspired to create the property while living on Lake Malawi, where they worked with the local community to found Katundu, an ethical artisan workshop, British owners James and Suzie Lightfoot designed the hotel with the discerning aesthete in mind. An ode to African artistry, it features unique pieces created by the 32 female artisans of Katundu, with an incredible chandelier crafted from tumbled glass, recycled copper disks, bicycle cogs, and clay beads commanding the lobby.

Furnished with hand-beaded textiles made from ostrich eggshells, cast bronze pendants, coconut shells and statement interiors crafted from old fishing boats, metal scraps and recycled glass, the hotel's colourful 32 rooms and three apartments evoke walking into a contemporary art gallery. Acting as an extension of the culture of Lusaka, Latitude 15° also works with Lightfoot Zambia – a local artist collective owned by James' sister, Gillie Lightfoot – to craft kitenge wall hangings, leather headboards, and upcycled antique mirrors, with visits to the centre arranged for guests upon request. Beyond the rooms, pre- and post-safari relaxation options abound, with two swimming pools, two bars, a spa, a 24-hour gym, and two restaurants to choose from. The property also has a co-working centre, The Works, as well as The Other Side, a networking and socialising hub with regular performances by local and regional entertainers.

ON YOUR DOORSTEP

A 20-minute drive from the hotel lies Lusaka National Park, Zambia's newest national park, which offers visitors an opportunity to spot over 1000 wildlife species during a game drive, from white rhino and giraffe to zebra and sable.

$ *Doubles per person: US$258*

🍴 *Contemporary European cuisine*

☛ *35F, Leopard's Lane, Kabulonga, Lusaka; https://15.thelatitudehotels.com. Latitude 15° is a 30-minute drive from Kenneth Kaunda International Airport, and is best reached by booking a private transfer through the hotel*

- Expert Talks
- Volunteering
- Workshops

LEARNING

ANDORRA

PROTECTING WILDLIFE IN THE PYRENEES

● Learn wildlife monitoring tactics from a professional scientist ● Monitor vegetation growth to gauge the effects of climate change ● Record diversity observations while trekking in the Pyrenees

If you love the idea of conservation voluntourism but don't know where to start, check out Earthwatch. The non-profit organisation connects travellers to environmental research projects focused on creating a sustainable planet. All trips are led by a professional researcher who assists volunteers in collecting data to aid studies on issues like climate change and ocean health. It's citizen science at its best, with research-oriented projects expertly guided to ensure results are scientifically sound and useful.

One such project is underway in the tiny European nation of Andorra, which straddles the border of Spain and France. Most of the country is situated in the heavily forested and often snowy Pyrenees mountains, which limits the scope for exploration and study. But Earthwatch's Wildlife in the Changing Pyrenees expedition aims to change that by engaging volunteers in wildlife observation, biodiversity sampling, and the monitoring and measuring of smaller plant and animal species. Mornings are spent in the field or at a research station before returning to a hotel in the evenings to review findings, enjoy Andorran cuisine, and do some light sightseeing or socialising before heading back into the field the following morning. There's also an optional day off for volunteers who want to explore the small ski resort town of El Serrat. You'll be hiking through the mountains while carrying gear on most days; expect a very active, challenging trip.

ON YOUR DOORSTEP
At El Serrat's nearby Ordino-Arcalis resort, you'll find skiing in the winter and mountain biking in the summer. You'll also be near the Sorteny Valley Nature Park, which has everything from hiking and forest bathing to a botanical garden and wildlife viewing.

$ *9-day Wildlife in the Changing Pyrenees project with Earthwatch Institute (www.earthwatch. org) all-incl US$2175*

🍴 *Andorran cuisine*

🚐 ***Earthwatch shuttles participants to El Serrat in Andorra from Barcelona (4 hours)***

BROWN BEARS OF THE PYRENEES

Efforts to reintroduce brown bears to the Pyrenees over the last 20 years have seen bear numbers climb from just half a dozen to around 40. But while this is great news for wildlife watchers, the programme is highly controversial among local farmers, who have blamed bears for an increase in attacks on sheep. Authorities continue to work alongside farmers to find a sustainable solution.

● **Expert Talks**   ● **Volunteering**

ANTARCTICA
SCIENTIFIC EXPEDITION CRUISE

● *Learn about Antarctica and the threats it faces during talks by renowned naturalists and prolific guest speakers* ● *Participate in citizen science activities*

There's no doubt that travelling to Antarctica generates more carbon emissions than the average holiday, but this shouldn't necessarily dissuade you from splurging on this trip of a lifetime.

With the planet's polar regions among the most susceptible to the effects of climate change, many leading scientists believe there's no place like Antarctica to reinforce the importance of limiting our impact. And while there are strict regulations for all expedition ships operating in the region, some are leading the pack. Among them, is Lindblad Expeditions. The inventor of modern expedition cruising, Lindblad has eliminated single-use plastics across its fleet, buys sustainable seafood, makes crew uniforms from recycled plastic and is building new ships that reduce emissions. It has helped to raise more than US$17million in donations for conservation projects, and in 2019, also became the world's first cruise line to become carbon-neutral. Guests on select expeditions are also invited to actively participate in research and conservation by taking part in a bioblitz (an intense period of biological surveying), adding another green tick to your trip.

$ *14-day trip with Lindblad Expeditions (www.expeditions.com) all-incl from US$14,680*

🍽 *Healthy international fare*

☞ *All cruises depart from Ushuaia, Argentina*

AUSTRALIA

BEACH CLEAN UP EXPEDITIONS

● *Learn clever new ways to lower your reliance on single-use plastics*
● *Help remove marine debris from Australia's most remote and beautiful beaches*

Australia's beaches might appear to be among the world's cleanest, but if you step off the beaten path, you might be shocked by what you find. This was the reality for Australian couple Nat Woods and Dan Smith, who launched not-for-profit lifestyle brand Clean Coast Collective in 2014 after a road trip around Australia opened their eyes to the devastating effect of plastic pollution on the nation's coastlines. Clean Coast Collective now leads periodic expeditions to help clean up some of Australia's most remote and polluted beaches, with a whopping 13.7 tonnes of rubbish removed to date.

Volunteers for each camping expedition – with all costs currently funded by sponsors – are selected following an application process which asks what you can bring to the expedition, from expert environmental knowledge to various creative talents, with participants encouraged to return to their communities after the trip to create a project to share their experience. Typically running for 10 days, expeditions are largely spent collecting and sorting rubbish, but there's plenty of fun to be had on the side, from nature walks to hanging out on the beach, to simply enjoying the digital detox. With few facilities at the off-grid campsites, volunteers gather around a crackling campfire each evening to share knowledge, and maybe a few tunes, over a well-earned vegetarian meal.

In late 2019 Clean Coast Collective was planning to expand its volunteering options to include women-only expeditions and corporate clean-up retreats, offering more opportunities to travellers keen make a positive influence, and learn about how you can make more sustainable changes to your everyday life.

$ *10-day expeditions with Clean Coast Collective (www.cleancoastcollective.org) are currently free*

🍽 *Healthy vegetarian and vegan meals*

☞ **Participants need to make their own way to the designated meeting point (typically Cairns), from where the group will travel to the clean-up site as a unit**

BONAIRE
REEF RENEWAL DIVING CERTIFICATION

● *Learn how to plant baby coral onto existing reefs* ● *Talk with experts about the role coral reefs play in ocean health* ● *Help with the foundation's underwater projects*

It's no secret that global warming, overtourism, and overfishing are affecting reefs around the world. In the Dutch Antilles, the Bonaire Coral Reef Restoration Foundation is doing its bit to reverse the damage. This non-profit organisation builds and maintains underwater nurseries for staghorn and elkhorn coral, which look somewhat like sunken Christmas trees. Once the corals are large enough, divers embed them onto living reefs. If you're a certified diver, you can spend three days with the foundation learning how to clean, prune, monitor, and replant corals. You'll then earn the PADI Reef Renewal Diver Specialty distinction, which allows you to

volunteer with coral restoration projects around the world. Nearby Harbour Village Resort has commendable sustainability initiatives and hosts a turtle conservation programme, though nearby Buddy Dive Resort is a more affordable option with its own eco-friendly projects, including a food waste donation programme.

ON YOUR DOORSTEP

The island of Bonaire has nearly 90 different dive sites, and dozens of excellent beaches provide the perfect base camp for a day of kayaking or stand-up paddleboarding. On the interior of the island, cave snorkel tours and birdwatching expeditions are popular with non-divers.

$ *3-day speciality diving certification with Reef Renewal Bonaire (www.reef renewalbonaire. org) US$330*

🍴 *Resort cuisine*

☛ **Most hotels are under 20 minutes' drive from Krajaliack**

BOTSWANA
OKAVANGO GUIDING SCHOOL

● *Soak up the knowledge of African bush experts* ● *Master the art of animal tracking, wildlife identification and more* ● *Learn essential skills to stay safe in the wilderness*

Looking for a deeper wilderness experience than a traditional African safari? On a seven-day bush skills course run by the family-run Okavango Guiding School, you can enjoy the same incredible wildlife experiences while simultaneously learning how to survive – and travel responsibly in – the African bush. From the ancient art of tracking to safe weapons handling, bird identification to approaching big game on foot, you'll learn skills that can be applied to wilderness adventures in Africa and beyond at the school's off-the-grid Kwapa Training Camp on the fringe of the World Heritage-listed delta. The

Okavango Guiding School is also southern Africa's only guide training school to sponsor a citizen on every course, meaning your participation contributes to creating meaningful career opportunities for local people.

ON YOUR DOORSTEP

Travellers keen to spend a bit more time in one of Africa's most incredible national parks can alternatively opt for a four-week nature guiding course that will help qualify you as a Level 1 FGSA (Field Guides Association of Southern Africa) Nature Guide.

$ *7-day bush skills course all-incl US$2122*

🍴 *Hearty African food*

☛ **Okavango Delta; www.guide trainingcourses. com. Rates include transfers from Maun, about 80 minutes' drive east**

COSTA RICA

Rancho Margot

● *Coach football or volunteer on community projects* ● *Take in twice-daily talks with experts in sustainability* ● *Sign up for workshops in composting, soap making, or Costa Rican culture*

Hammocks swaying in the wind, howler monkeys lazing in the trees, and colourful butterfly gardens: these are the obvious selling points of Rancho Margot, a completely off-the-grid eco-lodge near Costa Rica's Arenal Volcano. But behind the jungle retreat is a massive sustainable ranch, as well as a hydroelectric generator, a furniture workshop, and a bio-digester; some with living roofs.

For travellers who want to learn how the eco-ranch manages to be zero-waste, Rancho Margot offers a seven-day sustainable immersion programme. Guests sleep in rainforest bunkhouses and spend their days

learning about the facility's closed-loop system, from animal care and permaculture to holistic living and organic gardening. The programme includes all meals, twice-daily sustainability talks, and yoga classes in the ranch's riverfront, open-air yoga studio. Participants can also volunteer to coach football and help with community service projects in nearby La Fortuna and El Castillo, while travellers with teaching credentials can teach English.

Guests who are already skilled in sustainable development can apply for the volunteer programme, in which you'll work six days a week on the ranch in exchange for room and board. Volunteers will focus on hospitality (in cooking or housekeeping, for example), on the operation of the organic farm, or in a more specialised field, depending on your skill set. No matter how you visit, be sure to take advantage of the ranch's multi-level, spring-fed pool, heated with excess energy generated from the nearby rapids.

ON YOUR DOORSTEP
You'll be near all the adventure activities the volcanic region has to offer, from hikes through cloud forests to guided waterfall jumping expeditions – and don't forget about the nearby hot springs, said to be sourced from the same fountain of youth sought by explorer Ponce de León.

$ *6-night sustainable living immersion all-incl from US$695*

....

❍❚ *Organic, locally sourced Costa Rican and international cuisine*

....

☛ *Off El Fosforo-El Castillo Rd, El Castillo; www.ranchomargot.com. Rancho Margot is 3½ hours' drive northwest of San José. Rancho Margot can arrange transfers*

FAROE ISLANDS
Nature Preservation Project

● *Volunteer a long weekend to help build essential tourism infrastructure to preserve nature in return for a taste of authentic Faroe Islands hospitality*

With its dramatic coastlines, quaint turf-roofed houses and puffins galore, the Faroe Islands were bound to be 'discovered' sooner or later. Conscious of the effect of the dramatic increase in tourism to this 18-island archipelago, the self-governing Danish territory introduced a world-first sustainable tourism strategy in 2019 to help preserve it for the future.

For a long weekend in April coinciding with Earth Day, the volcanic islands were 'shut down' for maintenance work, with 100 people from 25 countries invited (via an open application process) to assist locals with tasks ranging from creating walking paths in well-trodden areas to constructing viewpoints to protect bird sanctuaries. In return, volunteers experienced a taste of local life by living and dining with locals. So successful was the project that the Faroe Islands decided to make it an annual event for as long as it's required.

ON YOUR DOORSTEP
Stay on to visit some of the sights that have helped to put the Faroe Islands on the tourism map, such as the incredible Mulafossue Waterfall on Vagar Island that gushes into the Atlantic, and the wild Vestmanna bird cliffs of northwestern Streymoy.

$ *The 3-day project is free*

|◉| *Faroe Islands fare*

☛ *Faroe Islands;* *www.visitfaroe islands.com*

GEORGIA

WINTER EXPEDITION TRAINING

● *Learn avalanche and self-arrest skills from alpine experts* ● *Build snow shelters and winter camps* ● *Practise survival techniques for below-freezing emergency situations*

Part of being a responsible traveller is being prepared for the adventure ahead. When you're not familiar with the local environment and how to travel sustainably within it, it's easy to accidentally cause damage, or put a strain on local communities and resources if you require emergency assistance.

Launched in 2015, UK-based adventure travel operator Secret Compass' Adventure Academy is designed to inspire regular travellers to get out of their comfort zone and learn the skills necessary to undertake extraordinary expeditions safely and responsibly. It takes travellers into some of the most remote environments on the planet to learn survival techniques; imagine learning how to navigate river crossings and administer first aid in the steamy jungles of Panama, or learning how to traverse the high alpine of the Caucasus Mountains in Georgia. The latter takes participants up Mt Kazbek, a remote, snow-covered volcano prevalent in Georgian folklore. The self-supported eight-day trip teaches skills like crampon and ice axe use, how to read and safely traverse crevasses, and how to move in avalanche-prone terrain during poor visibility. You might also have the chance to summit Mt Kazbek if the weather is favourable. It's a challenging adventure – there are no heated mountain huts to return to in the evenings and you'll be carrying all your supplies on your back – but you'll finish with a solid understanding of how to be a safer and more mindful high-altitude adventurer.

ON YOUR DOORSTEP
If you're keen to pick up a few souvenirs before you leave Tiblisi, skip the stores peddling mass-produced knicknacks in favour of independent design boutiques, such as Gallery 27 (N3 Betlemi St) and Ethno Design (23 Giorgi Akhvlediani St).

$ *8-day Georgia alpine skills expedition with Secret Compass (www.secretcompass. com) all-incl £1799*

🍴 *Backcountry cooking and dehydrated meals*

☛ **The expedition begins in Tbilisi, Georgia's capital, from where the group make the 3-hour drive to Kazbegi village**

GHANA
WOMEN'S ECONOMIC EMPOWERMENT TRAINING

● *Learn best practices for protecting marginalised women* ● *Teach public health in rural communities* ● *Run workshops and assist in educational programmes for Ghanaian women*

Countless studies have found that empowering women is key to sustainable development. This idea is so established that women's empowerment and equality plays a role in several of the 17 official sustainable development goals of the United Nations, including 'No Poverty' and 'Gender Equality'. In countries like Ghana, however, women are still often far removed from economic, educational, and political opportunities that could be harnessed to lift their communities out of poverty.

Travellers keen to help empower women in Ghana can sign up to volunteer at the Global Vision International (GVI) project near the beaches of Accra, which provides vocational and educational training for Ghanaian women. Volunteers will stay for up to 12 weeks working with local female-focused charities, or teaching public health or English classes, depending on your experience. With housing spread across several small towns, volunteers are immersed in community life, and on days off, there's plenty of time for wildlife viewing at nearby reserves, or perhaps even learning how to cook spicy Ghanaian food with locals (be sure to try fufu: mashed plantains with an aromatic, stew-y sauce.)

Known for its commitment to facilitating ethical and meaningful volunteering

opportunities in consultation with local communities, GVI trains all participants in vulnerable and adult protection. Volunteering scholarships are also available, and GVI provides guidance on fundraising.

ON YOUR DOORSTEP
Volunteers stay near the beach in Kokrobite, a relaxed seaside town. Within about an hour's drive, you can explore rainforests, laid-back beaches, historical sites, and the arts and cultural scene in Accra.

$ *Volunteer placement with GVI (www.giv. co.uk) per week incl lodging, transport and most meals per person from £238*

....

🍽 *Ghanaian and international*

....

☛ *The project is based in Kokrobite, about an hour by car from Accra; GVI meets volunteers upon arrival in Ghana*

ISRAEL

CENTER FOR CREATIVE ECOLOGY

● *Learn low-tech and affordable ways to provide food and shelter* ● *Help develop eco-friendly technologies for arid climates* ● *Soak up the expertise of desert permaculture pioneers*

A voluntary egalitarian society, Kibbutz Lotan (population 160) has turned its socially and ecologically conscious philosophy and its location in one of the driest human habitats on Earth into catalysts for innovation. To share their practical experience in desert living with the wider world and to develop and field-test new technologies, the kibbutz established the pioneering Center for Creative Ecology, whose motto is 'education for sustainability through hands, heart and mind.'

Inspired in part by progressive Jewish values, the centre, which is surrounded by the beauty of the remote Arava Desert, works to develop low-tech, low-cost solutions to the problems of food security, sanitation and limited water resources. Their hands-on educational programmes – including the Eco Experience, which mixes work on eco-projects with classes and demonstrations, and the Green Apprenticeship, a four-week course in permaculture design and sustainable engineering (US$2030) – offer people of all faiths and nationalities an opportunity to learn about ways to further social and environmental justice in the context of community building.

Participants learn how to create a biodiverse,

small-scale organic farm that uses compost to transform desert sand into nutrient-rich soil; construct sustainable buildings with eco-friendly materials such as straw bales and mud; and use simple, low-impact technologies to build bio-gas systems, composting toilets and kids' playgrounds made of cast-off materials. Participants live in the EcoCampus, a prototype neighbourhood of 10 geodesic domes where ideas for sustainable living – including a bicycle-powered washing machine – are trialled.

ON YOUR DOORSTEP
Kibbutz Lotan is 55km north of the Red Sea port of Eliat, whose reefs – especially those located within Eliat Coral Beach Nature Reserve – offer superb snorkelling and diving.

$ *4-day Eco Experience incl meals US$260*

🍽 *Participants help prepare healthy vegetarian and vegan meals*

☛ **Kibbutz Lotan, Arava Desert; www. kibbutzlotan.com/ cfce. The easiest way to get to the kibbutz is by taxi, but it can arrange pick-up from Lotan Junction, the closest bus stop**

JAPAN
Gankoyama Tree House Village

● *Learn how to chop wood, create a bow and arrow, and use rope to make a swing or hammock* ● *Practise yoga and build your own tree house*

On Japan's Bōsō Peninsula, 80km southeast of Tokyo, lies an old growth forest that feels a world away from the hyperactive capital. In 1998 Yoshinori Hiraga began to create an off-the-grid eco-village of tree houses here. It has since developed into a place for urbanites to reconnect with nature and learn some of the forestry skills of traditional Japan (such as how to climb a tree using a rope and a stick) while staying in simple but comfortable tree house rooms.

Gankoyama is a real-deal sustainable enterprise: electricity comes from solar panels and a wind generator, water is sourced from local mountain streams, and much of the food cooked on and eaten around campfires is foraged from the forest or made from locally grown ingredients. Mornings begin with sunrise yoga, breathing in the fresh forest air. Ahh.

ON YOUR DOORSTEP
Also on the Bōsō Peninsula, you can stay, via Airbnb, at Brown's Field (brownsfield-jp.com), an organic farm, cafe and shop, run by cooking teacher and writer Deco Nakajima and her husband, writer and photographer Everett Brown.

$ *2-day forestry survival skills course full board ¥10,000*

🍽 *Organic vegetarian*

☛ **Minami Bōsō-shi, Chiba-ken; www. gankoyama.com. The camp is a 2-hour bus or train ride from Tokyo; rates include pickup from nearby stations**

● **Workshops**

JORDAN
Beit Al Baraka

● *Try your hand at beekeeping* ● *Learn sustainable skills that can be applied at home* ● *Forage for unique ingredients in Jordan's highlands* ● *Master the art of Jordanian cooking*

Tucked up in far northwestern corner of Jordan, the small village of Umm Qais has traditionally received little benefit from tourism to the ruins of Gadara, an ancient Roman-Greco city typically visited on a day trip from Amman. But an innovative local community tourism project is working to change that by offering visitors a fantastic reason to spend the night, and upskill while they're at it.

The brainchild of Amman-based sustainable tourism company Baraka Destinations, Beit al Baraka is a charming three-room guesthouse (complete with handcrafted beds) that engages the local community to provide activities focusing on sustainable skills that can be applied anywhere. After filling up on a delicious organic breakfast, you might opt to take a crash-course in beekeeping or trek in the surrounding hills to forage for edibles, such as wild almonds, enjoying a taste of local culture in the process.

ON YOUR DOORSTEP
Dive deeper into the history of the ruins of Gadara – which affords spectacular views across the Sea of Galilee in Israel – with a local guide arranged by Beit al Baraka. You can also learn how to weave a basket or take a cooking class.

$ *Doubles per person US$100*

🍽 *Jordanian cuisine*

☛ **Al Mutanabbi St, Umm Qais; www. barakadestinations. com. Umm Qais is 110km north of Amman: take a bus to Irbid, where you change to a minibus**

LAOS
OCK POP TOK LIVING CRAFTS CENTRE

● *Discover how Lao women are weaving a new future* ● *Learn the art of naturally dyeing silk* ● *Take a textiles class with a master weaver*

A shining example of how empowering women is the ultimate driver of sustainable development, Ock Pop Tok (East Meets West) provides meaningful employment to more than 500 artisans around Laos while simultaneously supporting the preservation of artistic traditions.

A serene complex beside the Mekong, the social enterprise's Living Craft Centre welcomes visitors interested in learning more about Laotian textiles, with free 30-minute tours run throughout the day. You can also try your hand at dying a silk scarf, creating your own textiles under the guidance of a master weaver, and more. For multi-day classes, it's

worth booking a room in the attached Mekong Villa which is beautifully furnished with local textiles. Along with the excellent on-site Silk Road Cafe overlooking the river, it's committed to reducing its reliance on single-use plastics, with free water refill stations available.

ON YOUR DOORSTEP
Don't miss the not-for-profit Fibre2Fabric Gallery above the Silk Road Cafe. Dedicated to documenting and exhibiting textiles from around the country, including incredible heritage pieces, its exhibitions are presented in English and Lao.

$ *Doubles from US$75; half-day workshops from 208,000LAK*

🍽 *Lao cuisine*

☞ *Ban Saylom, Luang Prabang; www. ockpoptok.com. Just 2km from Luang Prabang, the centre is easily reached on foot or by tuk-tuk*

● **Expert Talks** ● **Volunteering** ● **Workshops**

MALAYSIA
BORNEO SUN BEAR CONSERVATION CENTRE

● *Volunteer at the world's only sun bear conservation centre* ● *Devise enrichment activities for orphaned bears* ● *Read up on sun bears, and prepare talks for visiting schools*

Orangutans might be Borneo's most famous mammal, but it's not the island's only wildlife species in crisis, with sun bears having declined by a whopping 30% in the past 30 years. For travellers keen to see the world's smallest bears stick around, Sabah's Borneo Sun Bear Conservation Centre (BSBCC) runs a volunteer program where you can make a real difference.

During a two- or four-week placement at the rehabilitation, education and research centre, volunteers conduct tasks ranging from designing and implementing enrichment activities for orphaned and ex-captive bears (such as hiding

food to encourage foraging behaviour) to educating visitors on threats to their survival. While you won't have direct contact with bears (for your safety as much as theirs), it's an incredible opportunity to spend quality time observing and supporting this incredible species.

ON YOUR DOORSTEP
Volunteers are also trained on how to conduct themselves in the company of wild orangutans. With the world-famous Sepilok Orangutan Rehabilitation Centre just next door, you're likely to encounter at least one of these critically endangered primates.

$ *14-day volunteering program MYR4690*

🍽 *Malay, self-catering*

☞ *Sabah; www. bsbcc.org.my. The centre is on the edge of Kabili-Sepilok Forest Reserve; project costs cover transfers*

NORWAY
ARCTIC CLEAN-UP
ARCTIC EXPEDITION

● *Get a taste of life onboard a research vessel* ● *Gather data about surface microplastics for ongoing research projects* ● *Clean beaches while participating in marine litter surveys*

Adventurous travellers who dream of exploring the frozen world of the Arctic on a more intimate vessel than a typical emissions-heavy cruise ship would be wise to look up Narwhal Expeditions. Named after the 'horned' whale native to Norway's icy waters, the company runs sailing trips in remote Arctic waters on a 15m-long yacht. Teams are always small, with just two crew members and four guests. Amenities land between basic and comfortable, and crewing isn't required if you don't know the difference between a jib and mainsail.

Narwhal Expeditions runs more than half a dozen expeditions throughout the year, but the most significant option is the Clean Up The Arctic research trip. Launching from Longyearbyen, Svalbard – the northernmost town in the world, where polar bears outnumber people – the two-week expedition sees volunteers conduct litter surveys, remove debris from beaches, and participate in marine mammal population studies along Svalbard's coastline, all while admiring the incredible seascapes and wildlife this deep corner of the Arctic is famed for. With research collected shared with non-profits and universities to inform policy decisions, assess ocean health, and further develop an understanding of the effects of climate change on Arctic food webs and ecosystems, participants can make a genuine contribution to science. While the crossing of the Barents Sea is a six-day slog of around-the-clock sailing, if the weather is favourable you may be able to stop at Bjørnøya (Bear Island) Nature Preserve along the way.

ON YOUR DOORSTEP
The mainland town of Tromsø, a popular destination for Northern Lights viewing, is the expedition's final port of call. Be sure to schedule a dinner at Restaurant Smak (www.restaurant-smak.no), which offers a Norwegian-inspired set menu showcasing local ingredients and flavours.

$ *13-day Clean Up The Arctic expedition with Narwhal Expeditions (www.narwhalexpeditions.com) £2999*

🍴 *Wholesome Scandinavian cuisine*

☛ **You need to fly to the island of Svalbard. Several flights run daily between Oslo and Longyearbyen. From the airport, it's a 5-minute drive to meet the crew at the Longyearbyen Harbour**

How to choose a
sustainable
volunteering project

The UN considers volunteerism indispensable to achieving its Sustainable Development Goals, though it's important to remember that not all volunteer-abroad programmes are created equal.

'To get the most out of volunteering you need to put effort into choosing who you go with and what you do,' says Dr Kate Simpson, an expert advisor on *Lonely Planet's Volunteer: A Traveller's Guide to Making a Difference Around the World* who has spent years researching and working in the international volunteering industry. These questions are designed to help you learn as much as possible about the quality, value and sustainability of volunteer projects before you dedicate your annual leave to one.

WHAT WORK WILL I BE DOING?

An organisation with a good volunteer programme should be able to tell you what sort of work you will be doing, including how many hours a day and how many days a week, and with which host organisation, well in advance of the project start date. A typical source of dissatisfaction for volunteers is not doing what they planned (and paid) to do.

DOES THE ORGANISATION WORK WITH A LOCAL PARTNER ORGANISATION?

If a volunteer programme is to be of value to a local community it should work in collaboration with, rather than be imposed on, that community. Find out who that partner is and how the relationship works. Is someone from the local organisation involved in the day-to-day management of your project? What sort of local consultation took place to build the project? Why is the project of value?

WHAT TIME FRAME IS THE VOLUNTEER PROGRAMME RUN ON?

A well-structured volunteer programme should have a clear time frame, and organisations should know from one year to the next whether a programme will continue. One-off programmes, and especially placements, can be problematic. If you are acting as a teaching assistant for a month, what happens the rest of the school year? Are other volunteers sent or is the placement simply ended? It may also be very disruptive for children to have constantly changing staff. Establishing the level of commitment an organisation has to a given project or placement is vital in establishing the quality, and therefore value, of that volunteer programme.

DOES THE ORGANISATION HAVE POLICIES TO SAFEGUARD LOCALS, WILDLIFE AND THE ENVIRONMENT?

All volunteer organisations should have a safeguarding policy for children and vulnerable adults whether they work with them or not, and programmes that work directly with children must include child protection training for volunteers. Similarly, high-welfare wildlife sanctuaries have policies to protect wildlife (restrictions on human-animal contact are common), with appropriate training provided to volunteers. Volunteer organisations should also be able to tell you how they work to minimise the environmental footprint of their programmes.

WHAT SUPPORT AND TRAINING WILL YOU RECEIVE?

Organisations offer vastly different levels of training and support. Look for an organisation that offers not only pre-departure training but also in-country training and support. Learning about both the practicalities of your volunteer job and the culture of where you are travelling to will help you get and give the most. Local support is also important, but ask if 'local' means just across the road or several hours away by bus. Make sure there is somebody in the country with direct responsibility for you. All projects require problem solving at some point and you will need someone on hand to help you with this.

DOES THE ORGANISATION MAKE ANY FINANCIAL CONTRIBUTIONS TO ITS VOLUNTEER PROGRAMMES? IF SO, HOW MUCH?

Volunteer programmes need funds as well as labour, so ask where your money is going, and be persistent about getting a clear figure, not a percentage of profits. Also, be aware that payments for your food and lodging often do not assist your volunteer programme.

WHY DO YOU WANT TO VOLUNTEER?

Don't forget to analyse your intentions for volunteering. Do you legitimately want to give back to the less fortunate, or are you more interested in seeking validation from your peers on social media or using the experience as career leverage? If you approach volunteering with the curiosity and humility to learn, you – and the project – will get much more out of it.

PAPUA NEW GUINEA
KABAKON KASTAWAY

● *Learn from locals how to survive on an uninhabited tropical island* ● *Weave traditional mats to take home with you* ● *Catch and cook your own lobster dinner*

Have you ever wondered if you could survive on a deserted island? Thanks to an award-winning tourism product offered by Oceania Expeditions, you can learn the art of living off the land on an idyllic island in Papua New Guinea in the ultimate low-impact cultural exchange.

Located in the Bismarck Archipelago in the nation's northeast, uninhabited Kabikon Island is used by the villagers on next-door Karawara Island as their garden isle. Here tropical fruits grow in abundance, taro and tapioca thrive under groves of coconut palms, and the surrounding seas swarm with seafood.

While staying in a traditional style thatched bungalow for four days, castaways will be visited by villagers from Karawara who will teach you the skills you need to be self-sufficient, from hunting lobster to cooking in a ground oven, making your own coconut milk to harvesting eggs from scrub fowl. You'll even be taught how to harvest natural materials to weave your own mat. Guests are then left to their own devices until the villagers' next visit.

Not only is it the ultimate opportunity to 'rewild' yourself while connecting with

local culture, the partnership provides an income stream for the local community and encourages pride in local traditions. If you play your cards right, you might even be invited to travel to Karawara to join a local family for dinner and learn the songs of the village.

ON YOUR DOORSTEP
The trip includes a recovery day at characterful Kokopo Beach Bungalow Resort on New Britain, which can arrange activities ranging from snorkelling and diving WWII wrecks to touring the nearby town of Rabaul, which was devastated by a 1994 volcanic eruption.

$ *5-night Kabakaon Kastaway experience with Oceania Expeditions (www. oceaniaexpeditions. com) AU$7970*

⦿I *Cook your own hunted and foraged produce*

☛ *Kabakon island, East New Britain. Participants must take a domestic flight from Port Moresby to Tokua Airport on New Britain island, where they'll spend a night in comfort before being dropped on nearby Kabakon island*

PERU

HUILLOC HEALTHY COOK STOVE PROJECT

● *Help to install healthy cook stoves to make life-changing improvements to remote Peruvian communities* ● *Gain an insight into Andean culture off the tourist trail*

In a remote corner of Peru's Sacred Valley, the small village of Huilloc relies on wood to burn in rudimentary open fire cook stoves. The stoves produce a thick smoke that hangs in the air, trapped within the confines of the small kitchens. Mostly it's the women and children who inhale the smoke during meal preparation, which, according to the World Health Organization, is linked to a whole list of health nasties from pneumonia in children to chronic obstructive pulmonary disease, low birth weight babies and lung cancer.

Inviting travellers to take an active role in giving back to locals, socially conscious operator World Expeditions' Huilloc Healthy Cook Stove Project sees guests spend two days installing healthy cook stoves into the kitchens of the village's 200 families. Staying in local homestays, guests are immersed in community life, with the opportunity to take in a traditional weaving demonstration, learn about the local farmers' connection to Pachamama (Earth Mother), and simply soak up the atmosphere of a traditional Peruvian village untouched by mass tourism. With a World Expeditions cook in charge of preparing delicious, hygienic meals, you'll get the fuel you need to complete the job, with your final afternoon free to explore the famous Inca ruins of Ollantaytambo, from where frequent trains leave for Aguas Calientes, the town at the base of Machu Picchu.

ON YOUR DOORSTEP

While you're wandering the alleys of Ollantaytambo, look out for guinea pig 'farms'. Some locals raise the rodent species in their own homes as a sustainable food source. For a small tip, they might even let you feed them.

$ *4-day experience with World Expeditions (www.worldexpeditions.com) including most meals AU$1130*

─────────────

|O| *Balanced international dishes with a Peruvian twist*

─────────────

☛ **Huilloc, Sacred Valley. Participants are picked up in Cuzco**

PORTUGAL

TERRA ALTA

● *Learn how to keep bees* ● *Master the art of zero-waste living* ● *Get accredited in permaculture design* ● *Absorb the expertise of guest teachers*

In a valley protected by old oak and cork trees, within earshot of the Atlantic, Terra Alta has been evolving as a permaculture education site for a decade. Its courses are the ultimate learning holiday: students sign up for two-week blocks of intensive workshops and talks, or month-long apprenticeships, and live on-site.

Natural building, food forestry, bio-intensive farming, natural bee-keeping and zero waste practices are covered, and the learning style is extremely hands-on, which also means mucking in with cooking and cleaning. Students of the two-week Permaculture Design Course leave with an accreditation from the UK Association of Permaculture.

Lessons, sometimes by guest teachers ranging from herbalists to bakers, are held both indoors and outdoors. Founders Pedro Valdjiu and Rita Seixas have spent years refining the design of their land to create a comfortable learning environment. 'All our structures are low-impact,' says Pedro. 'We try to use as little plastic and rubber as possible, though when we do we use upcycled materials as much as we can. Most of our buildings are made with cob (a mixture of sand, clay and water), wood and glass.'

Students camp in a shady spot in a Japanese-style wooden structure with compost toilets and warm-water showers fashioned from upcycled doors and glass. There's an ancient well on the site, drawing water from a natural stream, while a kitchen garden and herb spirals provide ingredients for group meals. This is sustainable, communal living with a smattering of comfort. Add night-time fire circles and pathways leading into the hills above Terra Alta for reflective moments, and it's about as dreamy as school can get.

ON YOUR DOORSTEP
Before or after your course, earmark some time for Sintra, where the Unesco-listed centre holds a colourful, much-photographed castle and whimsical gardens.

$ *2-week permaculture course all-incl from €850*

⦿I *Healthy, vegetarian and vegan home-cooking*

☛ *Sintra department; www.terralta.org. Take the train from Lisbon to Sintra, then catch the 403 bus from Sintra to Ulgueira (in the direction of Cascais). Terra Alta picks up from Ulgueira*

TAKE A HIKE

In 2019, Portugal's 700km+ network of hiking trails known as the Rota Vicentina (www.rotavicentina.com) was extended to include 24 circular routes that can be completed in half a day or less. The private non-profit association behind the Rota Vicentina works with more than 200 local businesses that share its sustainability goals, helping to promote sustainable tourism beyond Portugal's beach resorts.

● **Expert Talks** ● **Workshops**

SOUTH KOREA
TEMPLE STAY

● *Learn the secret to living with less from those who do it best* ● *Practise mindfulness during meditation sessions* ● *Craft your own traditional lotus lanterns and prayer beads*

As masters of minimalism go, it's difficult to beat Buddhist monks. In South Korea, an innovative company called Temple Stay offers a rare opportunity to learn the art of living more sustainably by immersing yourself in Korean Buddhist temple life for a weekend.

Overnight stays at any one of Temple Stay's partner temples around the country typically see guests spend most of their time meditating and chanting in the lotus position, and taking tea with monks between sessions. The evening meal (which can range from simple to gourmet) is eaten in silence to maintain mindfulness, with dinner usually followed by monastic music performances before temple guests make their way to simple communal sex-segregated sleeping areas.

Beginning with a silent dawn meditation session, the next day could see you hike into the surrounding mountains to visit shrines, or perhaps attend a prayer bead-making class intended as a sort of meditation in motion, with the beads serving as keepsake of your experience learning how to live – and thrive – on less.

$ *2-day programme with Temple Stay (https://eng.temple stay.com) all-incl KRW70,000*

🍽 *Broths and simple vegetarian dishes*

☛ *The Temple Stay program is available at more than 30 Buddhist monasteries around South Korea*

THAILAND

Sampran Riverside

● *Learn organic tips from Thai farmers in a laid-back riverside garden*
● *Visit organic markets to stock up on ingredients for spa treatments and cooking classes*

If you've ever fancied learning to plant rice on holiday, you've come to the right place. Sampran Riverside sprawls over 70 acres in a prime location beside the Tha Chin River, with accommodation in antique teak houses and Thai-style hotel rooms, but it's the organic ethos that is the main draw. The owners are passionate advocates of organic farming and its ability to free farmers from the financial control of agrichemical companies, and they are involved in a huge outreach program to convert local farmers to the cause. They're also passionate about involving guests in the process.

As well as running their own organic farm and buying tonnes of organic fruit, vegetables and rice from local producers, they offer immersive workshops in such farming practices as growing rice, harvesting pomelos and cultivating bananas, alongside interactive tours of local organic farms and farmers markets. You can even throw in a cooking course and learn some recipes to make with all the ingredients you learned to grow on the farm. Alternatively, after a hot morning toiling in the heat,

you might prefer to harvest some herbs for a traditional herbal massage back at the hotel. It's an active, educational experience that offers some surprising insights into farming life in Thailand, and plenty of inspiration to put your green thumb to good use back home.

ON YOUR DOORSTEP

To experience more of Thai life off the tourist trail, the Phuttha Monthon Buddhist Park is just west of the river, while the soaring, bell-shaped Phra Pathom Chedi and Sanam Chandra Palace are a short trip east.

$ *Doubles from THB2700*

🍽 *Organic Thai and international cuisine*

☛ *Km32 Pet Kasem Rd, Sampran, Nakorn Pathom; www.sampranriverside.com. Nakorn Pathom is 30km east of Bangkok, an easy trip by train from Thonburi Station, or by bus from Bangkok's Southern Bus Terminal*

UK
Bushcraft & Survival Training

● *Test your aptitude for foraging, shelter-building and wayfinding* ● *Learn survival skills from a mountaineer and endurance runner* ● *Master strategies that could save your life*

Foraging, fire-building, way-finding and water sourcing…Backcountry Survival's UK courses are the stuff Ray Mears fans dream of. But even everyday outdoorspeople can benefit from training that ultimately arms you with the skills to approach wilderness travel more responsibly. Founder Neil Foote grew up wild camping and careering through the woods around his home town of Fife in Scotland. He went on to become an ultra-marathon runner and mountaineer, and is one of the founding members of the UK's Survival Training Award Scheme. His courses (with one-day options also available) are rated according to their level of difficulty and designed to complement such outdoor activities as hiking, kayaking and cross-country skiing. Recognising that survival skills are often most needed when activities like these go awry, Neil's courses cover not just woodland training but also terrains such as lochs, upland, sea and rivers. At the most extreme, participants might be parachuted onto an island in the middle of a Highland Loch, Bear Grylls-style, without food and water. Softer options can cater for families, but all cover lifelines like what to do if you become stranded in the wilderness.

$ *3-day course from £210*

🍽 *Self-catering*

☛ **Northwest England and Scotland; www. backcountrysurvival. co.uk. Course venues range from survival in Scotland's Cairngorms to bushcraft in northern England and Wales**

UK
Forest Regeneration Volunteering

● *Learn about forest ecosystems from an experienced guide* ● *Propagate rare tree species at the charity's nursery* ● *Partner on projects with Scottish conservation organisations*

From deep blue lochs to dramatic, misty highlands, the landscapes of Scotland are legendary, but the introduction of non-native species and deforestation continue to wreak havoc on its natural beauty. Enter Scottish conservation charity Trees for Life which runs 'conservation week' programmes open to the public that aim to reset the balance. The excursions take volunteers into one of two key locations in Scotland to assist in reforestation efforts, but activities aren't limited to planting trees: you'll also work on wetland conservation projects, survey vegetation, and build tree guards to deter wild deer.

All projects are based in the Caledonian Forest, a lot smaller today than when the Romans gave it its name. The wilderness area is home to rare plant and animal species, including several found nowhere else in the British Isles. Volunteers work towards helping those critically threatened populations return to more stable numbers.

ON YOUR DOORSTEP
You'll have a day off during the programme to relax or explore the area. Nearby National Nature Reserve is a hiking haven, and the volunteering locations are about an hour from paddling and cycling routes around the famous Loch Ness.

$ *7-night programme all-incl £395 (www. treesforlife.org)*

🍽 *Vegetarian meals*

☛ **Glen Affric or Dundreggan, Scotland. Volunteers get pickups from Inverness train station**

USA
VIRGIN ISLANDS: RIDGE TO REEF FARM

● *Volunteer at a tropical organic farm* ● *Learn new sustainability skills while sleeping off-the-grid on a Caribbean island* ● *Sign up for workshops on bush skills, agroforestry and more*

Sleep in a solar-powered cabin (shared or private) on an organic-certified farm in the rainforest of St Croix and learn about its goal of feeding 1% of the US Virgin Islands' population healthy, local food (mostly through school lunches). Visitors can grab a self-guided interpretive map and tour the lush grounds, replete with community-supported agriculture fields, a tilapia pond and more. You can also get your hands dirty by volunteering in the field and cooking up your yield in the off-grid community kitchen.

Ridge to Reef maintains a busy calendar of events, including workshops on bush skills, permaculture, agroforestry and sustainable living. It also runs a Slow Down Dinner series where local chefs, fishers and farmers collaborate on a six-course meal and share stories of where the ingredients came from.

ON YOUR DOORSTEP
In nearby Frederiksted, chef Digby Stridiron is rescuing classic Crucian dishes and infusing them with modern touches at the West Indian kitchen Braata (braatastx.com). Nearly everything is sourced locally – a rarity on an island that imports 97% of its goods.

$ *3-night shared room per person US$165*

🍽 *Communal cooking*

☞ *2903 Ridge to Reef Farm Rd, St Croix;* *www.ridge2reef.org*

USA

ALA KUKUI

● *'Talk story' with native Hawaiians in Hana* ● *Join Hana's local families as they connect with innovative chefs to celebrate food and tradition* ● *Learn about the ancient art of hula*

Just off the iconic Hana Hwy, which traces the eastern curve of Maui, an intimate retreat centre sits nestled among the kukui trees that share its name. Ala Kukui is run almost exclusively by Hana-born Hawaiians whose history with the land goes back at least five generations. As a guest, you're brought into that history and invited to share in the very learning and practice that makes the Hawaiian spirit so special — and in a way that is typically inaccessible to visitors.

This isn't your typical commercialised hotel luau (Hawaiian feast). Here, there is no show. Though Ala Kukui offers guests a choice of studio apartment, four cabins, or main house that sleeps up to 14, all designed to highlight the beauty of the natural environment, its main purpose is to serve native Hawaiians, strengthening the Hana community by deepening cultural connection through storytelling, hula, cooking, and other traditions. Because the community dictates the experience – the invitation, the education, the programming – guests are privy to a depth of uncompromised craft. The best way to experience it: join one of Ala Kukui's cultural retreats, like the hula

retreat, which focuses on the three pillars of hula (spiritual, intellectual, and physical) in an intensive programme wherein you break from the ego, commune with the spirit, and connect with the earth through one of Hawaii's most celebrated (and often misunderstood) traditions.

ON YOUR DOORSTEP

Within a 3km radius of Ala Kukui, you'll find Hana Gold Chocolate to the northwest, which produces branch-to-bar goodies on one of Hawaii's first cacao plantations. To the north is Wai'anapanapa State Park, home to a black sand beach and verdant hiking trails.

$ *2-night stay for two from US$500*

I◉I *Cook your own in the shared kitchen*

☛ **4224 Hana Hwy, Hana, Maui, Hawaii; www.alakukui.org**

below & right: Earthship Biotecture & Academy

USA

EARTHSHIP BIOTECTURE & ACADEMY

● *Study botany, engineering and architecture under sustainability experts* ● *Help build an earthship for a non-profit organisation during your studies* ● *Learn the basics of sustainable living systems*

Sleeping in an earthship might sound like something reserved for astronauts, but these off-the-grid homes are very much of this world. Built with earth-friendly and repurposed materials, Earthships are powered by renewable energy, and even have their own greenhouses.

US architect Michael Reynolds first began pioneering eco-conscious building methods on a mesa northwest of Taos, New Mexico, in the early 1970s. Today, the site has evolved into a sprawling earthship community, with several of the futuristic buildings available for overnight stays. They range from cosy one-bedroom affairs to the Phoenix earthship complete with an indoor jungle, fish pond, and a Gaudí-meets-The-Flintstones architectural style.

If your interest in sustainable design extends beyond a weekend stay in upcycled hotel bliss, Earthship Biotecture has an immersive building programme. Over the course of a month, students learn the principles of sustainable design and how to engineer off-the-grid structures while studying under artists, engineers, and plant scientists. Academy sessions are held against the rosy backdrop

of Taos' mountains, as are the three-week internships; a secondary programme focused on ship building rather than principles of ship design. Academy accommodations are rustic, and you're in charge of feeding yourself, but did we mention you get to build an earthship?

ON YOUR DOORSTEP
Soak up the culture of nearby Taos, which has strong ties to both Spanish and Native American history. It's also one of the most popular mountain biking destinations in the Southwest, with extensive trail systems through the Sangre de Cristo Mountains.

$ *Earthships per night from US$140; 1-month academy excl lodging US$2500*

🍴 *Cook on-site, or dine in Taos*

☞ *2 Earthship Way, Tres Piedras, New Mexico; www. earthshipglobal. com. The Earthship Academy and visitors' centre are 20 minutes by car from Taos*

USA

LEAVE NO TRACE MASTER EDUCATOR COURSE

● *Learn the history of the 'Leave No Trace' mentality* ● *Help repair over-touristed areas at a Hot Spot event* ● *Develop plans to teach your own Leave No Trace classes*

Anyone who has ever been frustrated by hikers with poor trail etiquette or by finding evidence of human impact in the wilderness might want to sign up for a Master Educator Class, held in partnership with the Center for Outdoor Ethics. The COE was founded in 1994 but the idea behind the importance of thoughtful, zero-impact outdoor behaviour has been around for decades. The class teaches 'Leave No Trace' (LNT) ethics and how to facilitate your own LNT class after successful completion of the programme. The five-day classes are held across the country, so you can choose to learn in Washington's San Juan Islands or Colorado's Rocky Mountain National Park, among other wilderness locations. Expect to hike, camp, and paddle your way to a more responsible wilderness travel mindset.

For travellers with less time, the COE's Hot Spot events are another way to volunteer. These programmes allow volunteers to pitch in at one of the organisation's designated 'hot spots'; ecological areas particularly threatened by human recreation. Most events have only a few activities available to the untrained public, so contact the COE before making plans.

$ *5-day Master Educator Course prices around US$600*

|●| *Most programmes include camp-style meals*

☛ **Various locations across the USA; www.lnt.org**

INDEX

ACKNOWLEDGEMENTS

Sustainable Escapes

Published in March 2020
by Lonely Planet Global Limited
CRN 554153
www.lonelyplanet.com
ISBN 978 17886 8944 1
© Lonely Planet 2020
Cover image: © Timmy Page
Back cover image: © 2020, Beit Al Baraka
Printed in China
10 9 8 7 6 5 4 3 2 1

Managing Director, Publishing Piers Pickard
Associate Publisher Robin Barton
Commissioning Editors Dora Ball, Sarah Reid
Editor Sarah Reid
Proofreading Karyn Noble
Art Direction Daniel Di Paolo
Layout Lauren Egan
Print Production Nigel Longuet
Thanks to Cheree Broughton, Flora Macqueen, Simon Hoskins, Polly Thomas

Written by James Bainbridge, Joe Bindloss, Ian Centrone, Suzie Dundas, Ethan Gelber, Sarah Gilbert, Carolyn Heller, Martin Heng, Mark Johanson, Ria de Jong, Hannah Lott-Schwartz, Lorna Parkes, Sarah Reid, Simon Richmond, Daniel Robinson, Louise Southerden, Michaela Trimble, Tasmin Waby.

STAY IN TOUCH lonelyplanet.com/contact

AUSTRALIA
The Malt Store, Level 3, 551 Swanston St,
Carlton, Victoria 3053 T: 03 8379 8000

USA
Suite 208, 155 Filbert St, Oakland,
CA 94607 T: 510 250 6400

IRELAND
Digital Depot, Roe Lane (off Thomas St), Digital Hub,
Dublin 8, D08 TCV4

UNITED KINGDOM
240 Blackfriars Rd, London SE1 8NW
T: 020 3771 5100

Paper in this book is certified against the Forest Stewardship Council™ standards. FSC™ promotes environmentally responsible, socially beneficial and economically viable management of the world's forests.